Tip to Toe

A remarkable, true story of courage and determination.

To Les
With my sincere
best wishes
from
Swales

14ᵗʰ. Nov. '06.

Tip to Toe

A remarkable, true story of courage and determination.

Swasie Turner MBE

JEREMY MILLS
PUBLISHING LIMITED

Published by Jeremy Mills Publishing Limited
The Red House, 22 Occupation Road, Lindley
Huddersfield, HD3 3BD, UK

www.jeremymillspublishing.co.uk

First published 2006

ISBN: 1–905217–16–1

Book Design by Paul Buckley

Contents

Preface

THIS BOOK DEPICTS yet another 'first' by intrepid 'wheelchair pilot' Swasie Turner. It fully chronicles, in text and graphic illustrations, his epic wheelchair push in a standard NHS castered Lomax wheelchair from John O' Groats to Land's End. This length of Britain end to end fundraising endeavour took 44 days to complete the physically demanding 904.2 miles. His many adventures and encounters are both amusing and breathtaking.

Swasie's efforts are an illustration of his dedicated and total obsession to raise money for cancer research in memory of his loving wife Marjorie, who was cruelly taken from him by this horrendous disease. A loss that motivates his eccentric, never ending but highly successful fundraising exploits.

This book is an inspiration to all that venture through the pages of this truly fascinating publication.

In Loving Memory of my dear, beloved wife Marje, so cruelly taken from me by the scourge of cancer. Her loss I will never come to terms with.

I dedicate the privileged and honourable award of my MBE to 'my Marje', my true and inspirational heroine.

Dedication

TO THE FIREFIGHTERS (of *all* ranks) of each Brigade from John O'Groats to Land's End who fed, watered and provided accommodation for me and my backup team Art and Grant from Lomax, throughout the whole of my 'trek'.

I thank you all profusely from the bottom of my heart. The benevolence, extreme kindness, generosity and wonderful hospitality both from you and your families are without equal. You are *all* without doubt, ambassadors of the service.

I deem it truly an honour and a privilege to have been in your company and I am extremely proud to have made many new friends amongst your ranks. I salute each and every one of you. Without your assistance the whole venture could not have succeeded. Thanks also to Lomax Mobility for their logistical support and provision of backup crew and facilities. I also wish to thank and acknowledge the kind advice and assistance given by the various police forces concerned as well as Mrs Cilla George and fellow members of the 'Land's End & John O'Groats Company', for their tireless efforts, including the wonderful reception I received on arrival at Land's End.

I dedicate this book to *all* firefighters, past and serving, and also those tireless and selfless nurses and doctors and the wonderful staff at Jubilee House, Penrith (the home for broken firefighters) who continually fight to mend and counsel injured and maimed firefighters and their families.

God bless you all.
Swasie Turner MBE

Foreword

By Dame Tanni Grey-Thompson DBE. (World Olympics Gold Medalist wheelchair athlete)

WHEN I FIRST heard of Swasie Turner I thought this guy must be mad. Who on *earth* would want to push from John O'Groats to Land's End, and in a DAY CHAIR? For me this is something comparable to doing it in Wellingtons or at worst, in hob nailed boots!

The reason that he wants to put himself through this sort of punishment is nothing short of incredible, because many times he is not pushing on smooth or flat roads, but across country, up mountains and in some of the most inhospitable conditions that you could imagine, and this is day after day.

I have a huge amount of admiration for what Swasie is trying to achieve, he never sits on his laurels, but once one challenge is out of the way and you think that he may rest for a while, he is there looking for something else mad to do and it is always a joy to sit down over a cup of coffee with him and hear his stories about what happened on the last stage of his journey. Even more fun, just when you think it can't get any crazier he tells you about his next plan. And it is not just about what he is doing, none of this is for himself, all of his efforts raise money for a very worthwhile cause.

Good luck Swasie......You are an inspiration to every wheelchair user, there are many times you could have taken the easy way out, but you haven't.

Tanni Grey-Thompson DBE

TIP TO TOE

Chapter One
The Birth of an Obsession

Due to a gratuitous act of violence whilst serving as a Police Officer on the streets of Merseyside my life was turned upside down at a stroke. After 14 painful operations, which included *two* knee replacements to my shattered right leg, it was finally deemed necessary to amputate the leg high above the knee in November 1996. I have subsequently been confined to living my life on the seat of my pants from within the armrests of my standard issue NHS castered Lomax chariot.

Although, presumably like most others who have been suddenly put in such an unenviable position as this, I did start to vegetate and suffer self-pity, however, a chance remark by a fellow patient was to change my lethargic disinterest in life. As I sat there in the limb centre awaiting assessment, having been taken there from the ward prior to my hospital discharge, I was placed among a number of outpatient amputees. One of these, a man in his mid-sixties, pushed his wheelchair over to me and, gazing at where my right leg had once been he asked, 'How long have yer been like that son?' 'A week', I solemnly replied with a voice cracking with emotion. The old man then sighed and whined, 'Yer'll never get used to it yer know. I lost my leg five years ago an' I still can't get to grips with the loss!' I sat there in total desolation and thought to myself, 'That's ALL I need' then moved away to a secluded corner of the room. As tears of self pity rolled down my cheeks I looked towards the door. I desperately wanted the porter who had delivered me to the centre to come back and collect me to return me to the comfort and warm hospitality of my ward. I felt like an alien. I didn't want to be among 'cripples in wheelchairs'. I wanted to become oblivious to the very fact that I too was now one of them.

At this time, additional ingredients ensured that mega stress and depression manifested themselves with a vengeance. Having already lost my beloved career in the police force due to my horrific injuries, plus the traumatic loss of my leg I also had a more serious scenario to contend with. I had the additional worry of my beloved wife and lifelong sweetheart Marje having recently had to undergo surgery for breast cancer. Attempts to substitute my missing limb with a prosthesis were subsequently to prove unsuccessful. However, I deemed that the constant worry of Marje's predicament completely paled my own problems into insignificance. Although we *were* told that she was 'in remission', I continued to suffer acute anxiety over her condition.

Medication for my 'post traumatic stress' and severe depression did not help one jot to lift me from the depths of my utter despair. Marje and I had been together since were both 14 years of age and had enjoyed 40 years of blissful marriage. We had our 'trials and tribulations' that ensure solid foundations to all successful marriages, as well as our having to contend with the traumas and numerous injuries sustained during my service with both the Fire Brigade and the Police Service. Now however there was the *ultimate* trauma – Marje's illness.

Due to the comments of the 'Job's Comforter' that day at the limb centre, I decided that I must do my *damndest* to see what I could do to assist in the fight against the ruthless and indiscriminate killer, *cancer*. I wanted to do this to say a BIG thank you for my Marje being saved from its fiendish clutches.

Although I had been strongly advised by the medics to 'take things easy for the first twelve months' after my amputation, to allow things to knit and heal, I decided to get out and about in my castered 'tank'. Having been blessed with a fair amount of upper body strength due to my involvement with weightlifting and boxing over the years, I didn't find it difficult to propel my chair along the roads of Wirral.

From very early on I realised the advantages of staying on the road! Unfortunately our pavements are *not* very wheelchair friendly due to high kerbs and lack of access slopes. Also, they are all too often littered with broken glass or liberally coated with dog filth, spit or other equally unsavoury infectious material to contaminate one's hands via the chair's wheels. There is also the ever-present risk of being run down by the many moronic pavement cyclists that abound. No, I considered it far *safer* to travel on the road! Ironically, very rarely did I, or have I, experienced irate motorists due to my presence on the highway, although I concede there have been one or two selfish and inconsiderate individuals. However, the majority of road users have been both friendly and willing to share the carriageways with me.

So, since my confinement to the chair in February 1997, I became dedicated to raising funds for the 'Cancer Gene Appeal' (now renamed the 'Clatterbridge Cancer Campaign'). My first endeavour came about due to my being asked one day as I trundled along the road, 'Are you training for the Wirral Walk?' At that time I was ignorant of what the 'Wirral Walk' was. My subsequent enquiries however revealed that this was a very popular annual event, which drew large crowds of fundraisers to raise money for various charities of their choice. The 'walk' is intended for *walkers* (not for hand propelled wheelchairs!) to complete the 15-mile trek from Seacombe Ferry in Wallasey along the rugged coastline of the Wirral peninsula to Thurstaston on the banks of the river Dee. The route is mainly across difficult terrain and includes sandy beaches, stiles and narrow footpaths.

I decided to have a go and attempt the long distance trek in my trusty chariot. This would be a challenge to say the least as no one had completed this event in such a standard conveyance under his or her own power unaided. Marje tried to dissuade me from entering for the event and the event's powers that be also considered my attempt would prove unsuccessful. After persistent requests and assurances as to my ability to complete the course, I was finally allowed to enter.

Subsequently, on Sunday, 11th May 1997 I took part and successfully completed my first 'long distance' wheelchair push to begin what was to become my life's total dedication, to raise money to fight the horrendous disease – cancer.

During this, my first endeavour, I raised over £200!

As time went on I became more and more eccentric in my fundraising endeavours. Trips of longer and longer distances and duration were undertaken – and successfully completed. These distances often surprised the many doubters that they could be done. Money (and notoriety) manifested itself, as well as valuable publicity, which was a major 'vehicle' to help generate the all-important funds.

My fundraising eccentricities became widely known. My endeavours aroused the interest of the 'after dinner circuit' and engagements followed which in turn generated more money for my 'bucket'. My 'After Dinner' talks then started to become a regular, additional source of my fundraising 'income' which has gone on to continually fill my engagements diary.

Alas, after only eight short months had elapsed, just as I was coming to terms with my unenviable 'new' way of life, my world fell apart at the seams.

A particularly virulent and aggressive form of cancer suddenly reared its ugly head and attacked my Marje with merciless ferocity. Within five short weeks my beloved wife and long standing best pal, when I needed her most, was to succumb to this scourge and die in my arms. I was, and will *always* be, totally devastated and inconsolable. My grief and bitterness at such a cruel and utterly soul destroying blow now manifested itself into a burning anger. I wanted vengeance! I was so distraught I wanted (and I can't deny I was tempted) to do something about joining her, such was my deep depression and inconsolably acute grief. However, Marje too would be devastated if she knew how I was thinking and what my intentions were. I decided to 'seek vengeance' by assisting the fight to eradicate cancer, the thieving assassin who took her from me. The deep love of my Marje, (my 'child bride') would now inspire my drive to fight this ruthless and indiscriminate killer. I now had an insatiable appetite to eradicate the scourge by *any* means whatsoever. My eccentric endeavours to raise money for this fight had now become a dedicated and total blind OBSESSION. This obsessive *crusade* will remain with me for the rest of my life.

It is this which has enabled me to swell the coffers of my 'bucket' via endeavours which many had considered would be impossible. My constant, solo 'fight' has caused me to have completed over 33,500 miles since my wheelchair confinement in February 1997 which in turn has generated *many* thousands of pounds for the Cancer Gene (Clatterbridge Cancer Campaign) Appeal and other worthy causes.

These endeavours have included climbing lighthouses and the infamous Blackpool Tower as well as the notorious Wallace Monument at Stirling, *all* with my trusty wheelchair! They also include many non-stop, long distance pushes of 41 miles from North Wales to Wirral, then a non-stop 72 mile, 20 hour circuit around the whole of the Isle of Anglesey. These were later followed by the completion of the infamous Isle of Man TT Circuit of 38 miles. Other equally lengthy jaunts were completed including the 'Great North Run'. All of these *unequalled* wheelchair endeavours *still* remain standard wheelchair 'firsts'.

My lengthy wheelchair climbs and pushes finally led me to what would be the *ultimate* of all firsts – that of pushing my standard Lomax chair, unaided, the whole length of Great Britain from John O'Groats to Land's End, the 'Holy Grail' of all efforts.

Again many 'doubting Thomases' expressed their lack of belief that this could be done in such a conveyance as an ordinary, standard wheelchair with front casters. However, they hadn't taken into consideration the fact that my Marje, is, and will *always* be, my *total* inspiration. In no way would failure be an option, I was as determined as ever and decided that I would 'go for it'!

Chapter Two
Obstruction at the Starting Line

THE CLATTERBRIDGE HOSPITAL Cancer Gene Appeal (the Clatterbridge Cancer Campaign) is based at Bebington, Wirral and is one of the country's leading establishments for oncology treatment and research. It is also the hospital where my beloved wife had been treated, nursed and cared for by those wonderful 'angels' of the nursing and medical professions.

In an effort to enhance funds for 'my' *number one* charity, I applied to enter the 1998 London Marathon 'fun run' with my standard wheelchair. I emphasised that in no way did I wish to enter the 'Wheelchair Race', I just wanted to partake in the event to raise money for 'my' charity. My application was refused! I made enquiries as to why I had been turned down and spoke to a Mr Alan Storey. The *able-bodied* Mr Storey informed me that 'he' considered that I would be physically *unable* to complete 26 miles in such a conveyance which was only constructed and intended for use around the house or wards, or perhaps for somebody to push its occupant to the local shops. What bloody cheek! I pointed out to Mr Storey that I had completed non-stop distances in excess of 26 miles on *many* occasions over all sorts of terrain. However, my comments fell on deaf ears.

Mr Storey did not deter me however and I continued to pursue my application to enter the prestigious event with the utmost vigour. I did not intend to give up lightly a chance of a lifetime to generate a lot of money for my 'bucket', not to mention the possible publicity which could well generate more cash in the future. I contacted the Minister of Sport, the late Mr Tony Banks, in an effort to facilitate my entry into the Marathon. The kind and courteous minister tried to assist my application but, again, my application was refused. Even the veteran marathon fundraiser Sir Jimmy Saville came to my aid and voiced his opinion that I should be allowed in. As Sir Jimmy Saville stated, if I were to start at the back *behind* the event's participating masses, how on *earth* could I be a danger to athletes who would be starting at different, distant venues? Also, the elite runners and wheelchair racers themselves started separately at *prior*, staggered times, again before the main body of thousands were to set off.

The event is supposed to be '*the Peoples' fun run*' which is intended for the raising of funds for their chosen charities. The media became involved and both Mr Storey and myself were interviewed on air (separately) as well as by the press.

To assist my efforts to take part in this prestigious event a local man, after becoming aware of the difficulties I was encountering, decided to voice his own sentiments to the press. The man, a veteran marathon runner who had completed the London Marathon 18 times as well as having completed the Paris, New York and most other major countries' marathons then volunteered what he considered to be 'unsavoury' information regarding *his own* experiences with the London Marathon. He mentioned various points that caused the media to take a keen interest into how the event is conducted. I was again interviewed as was the Marathon 'veteran'. The outcome of the media involvement and whatever this revealed has never been published.

I again applied to take part in the year 2000 event. *Again* my application was turned down. This time Mr Storey told the BBC that 'Mr Turner is the author of his own destiny and he didn't do his cause any good by refusing to take part in a lightweight racing type chair as advised'. This was now a completely new tack! At *no* time whatsoever had I *ever* been advised, requested or instructed to take part in any such type of wheelchair. Mr Storey emphasised to the press and media that my own chair not only would not be able to complete the distance, but if I did take part in it I would be 'a danger to others'. Mr

Storey elaborated by saying that I would 'run down' runners (in a chair that cannot travel at a pace over three to four mph!).

This time, the new Minister for Sport, Kate Hoey kindly tried to assist my endeavours. Again, her effort did not bear fruit and my participation was again thwarted. However, my persistent efforts would continue. I would become a 'thorn in the side' of the Marathon authorities due to my relentless efforts to take part as I considered it my *right* to do so. My sole intent was to take part purely to (a) raise money for my charity and (b) hopefully to be an inspiration to others who might just sit 'vegetating' at home in their standard chairs similar to mine, as I once did! This would certainly *not* be the end of my attempts to enter the London Marathon Fun Run, nor would I be forced to take part in any event whatsoever in anything other than my *standard* NHS Lomax wheelchair!

Chapter Three
'End-to-End' Venture — The Conception

DURING MY DISPUTE with the London Marathon authorities I continued to raise funds by my various 'unorthodox' ventures. I had by now started to become involved with assisting my wheelchair's manufacturer, Lomax of Dundee by 'projecting' their name and their product's endurance capabilities. I started to 'assess' and 'test' their standard chairs as I travelled new frontiers in my ongoing quest to raise money for 'my cause'. My travels involved negotiating tracks, heaths, commons and even shorelines, not the usual venues for such conveyances. I started to receive encouragement, assistance and valuable advice from Lomax which continues unabated to this day.

I was subsequently invited to attend a 'Mobility Roadshow' at Crowthorne near Reading by Mr John Wilmot the Chief Executive of Lomax (as by now I was more or less the unofficial wheelchair 'test pilot' for my host). John, his family and myself had by now established a firm, close and everlasting friendship which I value very much indeed.

Consequently, in June 1999 together with my 'mentor', carer, minder *and highly efficient photographer* Chris (affectionately known to all as 'Matron'), I attended the three-day event. It is Chris who transports me to the various fundraising venues where she then photographs the event for inclusion in my illustrated talks and any later publications. The majority of the pictorial contents of a previous, highly successful publication, *Wheelchair Pilot* are the product of Chris's skilled endeavours with the camera. The purpose of such a high profile event as Crowthorne is to create a 'shop window' for manufacturers. It is to enable various manufacturers, agents and companies who exclusively cater for the needs of the disabled, to advertise and exhibit their highly innovative products. I took a number of copies of *Wheelchair Pilot*, which fully illustrates my fundraising exploits, to exhibit on the Lomax stand.

During the three-day gathering, a television film crew were filming various aspects of the numerous types of equipment on display. One of the crew, Miss Lou Birks noticed my book. As Miss Birks leafed through the pages she became fascinated with the book's illustrated contents. The lady stated that not only did she wish to avail herself with a copy of *Wheelchair Pilot* but she was considering making a filmed feature of my endeavours sometime in the future. As the crew stood chatting to the management and staff at the Lomax stand, Miss Birks turned to me and casually asked what my *ultimate* ambition would be. I informed her that my ultimate ambition would be nothing more than to push my chair from John O'Groats to Land's End.

My comments brought ribald remarks and peels of laughter as some expressed their amusement at someone wanting to attempt what they considered to be an impossibility, especially in such a *standard* chair as mine. Lou kindly and politely reminded me of the enormity of such a dream. There were the Scottish Highlands, the mountainous steep climbs and descents, ongoing freezing inclement weather and stamina-sapping, lengthy hills both up, and down, for extremely long distances, she pointed out. I acknowledged their polite disbelief and accepted that although I would *like* to do it, I did however concede that the impossibility would not be due to my physical inability, but *purely* due to there being no back-up vehicle or logistical facilities. I went to great pains to emphasise it was only *this* problem which would prevent me undertaking such a venture which I was confident I could and *would* complete given half a chance!

As this conversation was going on, a quiet and extremely pensive Mr Wilmot (the Lomax Mobility Chief Executive) stood amongst us listening acutely to all that was being said. His left arm was folded across his broad, barrel of a chest and his right hand was held to his face as his index finger stroked his chin. After much thought and

John Wilmot and Crew at Mobility Roadshow

pensive deliberation Mr Wilmot suddenly turned to me and said for all to hear, to their utter astonishment, 'If you really think you could do it Swasie, Lomax will supply the back-up vehicle and cater for the logistics'. To say I was dumbfounded was to put things very mildly indeed. I was however extremely elated. Here was the absolute chance of a lifetime to attempt the ultimate of wheelchair 'firsts', this would be the *ultimate* of marathons, I couldn't believe it!

Without hesitation I replied, 'Okay, let's make a decision here and now, I'll set off from John O'Groats on Marje's birthday next year – 12th May'. All eyes turned to Mr Wilmot. 'DONE' he said without any hesitation and offered me his hand to 'shake on it'. This I accepted with an instant response, grabbing his outstretched hand and pumping it vigorously.

Having been a fully operational and experienced front line firefighter I decided to approach the Fire Service with a view to sharing funds raised during, and resulting from, the push between 'my' cancer charity and those of the 'Fire Services' National Benevolent Fund'. I would also ask them if they would provide overnight accommodation for my back-up man and me as we travelled the length of the two countries. The venture's commencement date was 11 months away and although it seemed an age away, there would need to be a lot of preparation and hard work to be done before then to enable this, the most unusual and ultimate of marathons to be successfully arranged.

However, with the backing of such big establishments like Lomax and the Fire Service, as well as the all important assistance and advice from the 'End-to-End' Authorities which would *have* to be enlisted, this venture could now become a viable venture. Could such a mammoth, physically demanding feat such as this be accomplished via such a basic conveyance – and, would *I* be up to such a challenge? Only time would tell!

There weren't so many sceptics in the little group now! Television's Lou Birks stated her intention to monitor the forthcoming venture's progress with the utmost vigour.

Consequently, the *'Tip to Toe'* wheelchair push in a standard Lomax chair was conceived. During the following months the birth of the venture would be awaited with bated breath.

Chapter Four
Faith and Charitable Benevolence –
Some (of the many) Who Gave.

MANY LENGTHY AND audacious negotiations ensued during the following months. The various (and many) Fire Brigades whose areas I would be travelling through had to be contacted. Requests to each Chief Officer would have to be made seeking their assistance and blessing. Overnight accommodation (and food if possible) would be sought at fire stations en-route. This would also involve contacting the many retained (part time) personnel, which in itself would be no easy task due to their various full time roles. This illustrates the administrative complexity involved in the arranging of such a high profile venture, which, let us not forget, would entail travelling through two 'countries'! Chief Police Officers would also have to be contacted and informed of the little 'posse' that would be wending its way through their 'patches'. This would be absolutely necessary both as a matter of etiquette and courtesy as well as seeking their blessing and their much valued help and guidance.

All in all, preparing for such a trek as this, as well as the logistical operation involved, would be no easy task for all concerned. Safety must and *would* be paramount at all times. Regular food and drink supplies would also have to be arranged for my back-up and myself.

Lomax would furnish a vehicle and driver as well as a spare wheelchair and component parts (which were never required). They would also furnish me with a brand new standard chair (identical to my own day to day chair) namely a standard, front castered NHS issue chariot. It would not in *any* way be a lightweight, 'gimmick bearing' rocket. It would not even have the luxury of brakes and steering other than the usual *locking* brake as on all chairs. On completion of the trip the chair would be given a place of honour at the 'end-to-end' museum, namely the Exhibition of Epic Journeys at the Miles of Memories Tourist Centre at Land's End. All would be wonderful! – so long as such a voyage into the unknown could be successfully completed by a (hopefully not overconfident) disabled *60 year old* ex-firefighter and ex-cop.

The provision of the vehicle and driver for the anticipated six weeks of the trip's duration, spoke volumes for both the confidence that Mr Wilmot must have had in me and also the extremely financial benevolence of Lomax. The cost of such provision would no doubt be astronomical due to the drivers' wages and potential of their numerous hours of overtime working and expenses that would be involved. Another financial burden would be due to the fact that the vehicle would be out of delivery service as well as the extremely heavy fuel bill that would be incurred as it crawled at walking pace during the lengthy six-week period.

Next, the expertise, help and guidance would need to be sought from the Land's End to John O'Groats Company. This association is the official body concerned in the authenticating of such marathons undertaken from 'end-to-end', one end of Britain to the other. Mrs Cilla George was very kindly ready and willing to give such invaluable advice and assistance on behalf of the Company. Without such assistance it is doubtful if such a venture could have taken place, let alone succeeded, as her knowledge, skills and kindness would prove to be priceless. (Cilla's kind and efficient administrative virtues eventually were to illustrate just *how* good both her and the association were, at the conclusion of the trek at Land's End!) Also, the push would have to be documented and endorsed en-route by various authorities to verify and authenticate the miles completed at regular periods. Forms would be stamped by Police, Fire, and Local Councils as this would eliminate the possibility of cheating. This procedure was very strictly monitored (and rightly so) by the Land's End to John O'Groats Company to ensure there were no false claims by some who may claim to have completed the lengthy journey by various means.

During the time that everyone concerned in the preparations were consuming copious amounts of headache pills (and no doubt I was the cause of their premature Valium addiction!), I was out completing my daily, 15 to 20 chair-borne mileages along the highways and byways of Wirral. I had the easy bit to do as the 'hive of backroom activity' continued relentlessly on my behalf! I did however start to increase the cost of my telephone bills enormously as I cheekily rang everyone I could think of to inform of my 'trek' and to hopefully seek their financial involvement. My audacity paid off considerably as the majority of my calls brought a kind and ready response in the way of assistance in one form or another.

The massive resources of **DURACELL Batteries**, via the charming and helpful Olivia Gregory were to assist Lomax in the venture. Their kind and untiring physical and financially generous assistance proved to be invaluable.

Other big household names that 'came aboard' were **Fuji Films**. They continually and unhesitatingly provide free film to furnish a pictorial record of my endeavours and this epic venture was to be no exception.

Jabra Europe, manufacturer of the highly efficient, robust and totally reliable mobile phone 'Hands Free' set, kindly provided me with one of their top of the range models, which I was to use throughout the whole of my trek. Even during heavy downpours and continually inclement weather, especially in the meteorologically temperamental Scottish Highlands, the equipment was to prove faultless. During the trip I would be constantly 'Live' on air via this product to various radio stations as well as numerous national and local press establishments. Except for the occasional 'blind spots', reception and transmissions would be perfect at all times.

Others who would willingly dig deep into their pockets or resources to furnish various forms of financial or materialistic assistance ranged from well known household names to small 'corner shop' businesses; each one's generosity being proportionate to their individual capabilities. Some of the *many* names that didn't hesitate to assist my quest for backing and oblige in one way or another include:

Vauxhall Motors the international motor manufacturer, Ellesmere Port, Merseyside, who were to give a substantial financial donation.

Greentyre whose (unchanged) tyres would cushion my journey for the duration.

Lucozade & Liptonice Tea each of whom were to provide copious amounts of their energy and stamina enhancing drink.

SIS (Science in Sport) who would supply highly nutritious food and drink.

Berghaus who would provide a sleeping bag and backpack drink dispenser.

Convetech Medical Supplies

Tempormed Medical Products

Penkeths Office Furnishers, Bebington, Wirral. (Who regularly donate cash).

AGA who also regularly donate cash to the Cancer Gene Appeal.

Mr John Birtwistle of Wirral Champion Magazine

Police News Fire News & **NHS News** (Britain's emergency services
National Newspapers).

Halfords Cycles, Inverness. They would repair my faulty (and supply a spare) Mileometer free

Morrisons Superstores, Cheshire.

Moreton Shoe Repairs, Wirral.

The Bike Shop, Moreton, Wirral.

Hoylake Cycles, Wirral.

Bosun's Locker, Hoylake, Wirral.

Toledo Camera Company, West Kirby, Wirral, whose proprietors Mr Martin Middleton and Mrs Ruth Johanson presented me with a high quality camera (with their compliments) to enable me to furnish an illustrated chronology of my venture.

Caldy Signs, Greasby, Wirral who were to furnish my 'advertising' flags.

Copydex Adhesive, Winsford, Cheshire.

Cateye – Zyro, Harrogate – Lights and mileometer.

The list of those who were prepared to back me became endless. Also, I must not forget all those generous people, including school children, who so regularly stop me and give me money as I continually travel along the roads of Wirral (in all weathers) irrespective of whether I am *officially* collecting or not. I am continually being inundated with copious amounts of kindness and selfless benevolence from people of all ages *every day*. Such wonderful, donating benefactors consist of my local bus drivers, taxi drivers, motorists, motorcyclists, cyclists and pupils travelling to and from their schools. Also included are the many householders and shopkeepers who come out to give generously to my obsessive cause. I am totally, profusely and *very* humbly grateful to each and every one. I thank each and every one who have, and continue to have, faith in my fundraising endeavours. I wish to thank all of the people who were to contribute and assist my 'end-to-end' venture as the big day of the push's start approached. We were now starting to 'line up for take off'!

Chapter Five
Final Preparations 'Set in Stone'

As PREPARATIONS STARTED to gather momentum I continued to feed the Cancer Gene Appeal fund via 'after dinner' engagements. As I scrutinised my diary one day I realised with horror that I was to give an address to the Allastock Ladies' Luncheon Club on Wednesday, 17th May 2000. The very attractive venue was situated in the beautifully picturesque 'green wellies' area of Knutsford in rural Cheshire. I immediately contacted the club's president Mrs Jean Bellamy in the hope of rearranging the date of my talk.

Alas, although a very sympathetic Mrs Bellamy understood my dilemma she informed me that arrangements had unfortunately been finalised and all invitations had been sent out to the club's members. Fortunately for me, my big 'take off' day was still some way off and I was able to rearrange the starting date of my trek by putting it back one week. The event was now scheduled to start on 19th May, seven days after Marje's birthday. It was anticipated that the long 'push' from John O'Groats to Land's End would take approximately 44 days – *if all went to plan*.

Another unique feature of the event was the brainchild of the innovative Mr Wilmot. He catered for the whole project to be available on the Internet Website via the address www.lomaxmobility.com. Here again was another first for the enterprising Lomax establishment. Mr Wilmot and his team also arranged banking facilities for the safe depositing of the anticipated reception of cash donations during the whole route. This would enable my crew to regularly deposit any sums received and would eliminate the risks involved with collecting cash.

CHAPTER FIVE – FINAL PREPARATIONS 'SET IN STONE'

Everything was going smoothly and we were now fully committed and on course for the epic adventure and trip of a lifetime to take place. It was now 'all systems go' and final preparations were at last set in stone.

Chapter Six
Birth of an Epic – Journey of a Lifetime

EVENTUALLY, AFTER MANY months of sheer hard work and no doubt many hours burning of the 'midnight oil' by the trip's various organisers, the time arrived to put the (wheelchair's) wheels in motion! In the meantime I had busied myself constructing an 'advertising mast' to fit to my chair. The mast had been donated to me by '*Hoylake Cycles*' of Wirral. The brightly coloured and adhesive plastic material from which I would make the pennants was kindly given by '*Caldy Signs*' of Greasby, Wirral. Each highly visible pennant would display the name of an individual organisation or business that had assisted or donated to the venture.

During the week prior to the start I received a telephone call from Lomax informing me that Art Sangster, my driver, would be outside my door at 5.00 a.m. the following Thursday when he would collect me and transport me up to Dundee for the *official* send off at 11.00 a.m. that same morning, prior to us travelling on to Wick.

Consequently, fully 'booted and spurred' I was waiting at my open front door for Art's arrival on the day. At dead on 5.00 a.m. the ever punctual Art arrived with his Lomax van at my gate. Lomax had taken a lot of trouble to furnish an extremely attractive and highly professional, informative and eye catching livery on their vehicle. Both sides bore information of the trip together with their internet address (which would provide daily, illustrated updates during the entire trip). The vehicle was a very impressive sight indeed. Inside was a large board, which would be fitted onto the outside of the vehicle covering the whole of the rear, bearing flashing lights and a warning to road users in large letters that a 'slow moving wheelchair' was ahead. Lomax had not spared *any* effort whatsoever to ensure that safety was paramount for this operation.

A subsequent and final check was made to ensure that nothing essential had been left behind then Art and I set off on our long journey to Dundee. After a pleasant and uneventful trip Art's pedantic navigation finally took us to the Lomax factory approximately five hours later. Shortly after our arrival a television camera crew arrived together with the press. The gathering was then graced with the arrival of Lady Provost of Dundee. The Civic lady had taken the trouble to come and wish me 'Bon Voyage'. Her presence and extremely kind gesture made me feel very humble *and* very privileged indeed. Mr Wilmot's attractive wife Careen furnished a wonderful and varied buffet to enhance the occasion further. We were all then invited by our hosts into the Lomax Boardroom to enjoy the mouth watering and more than generously adequate fare and celebratory toasts.

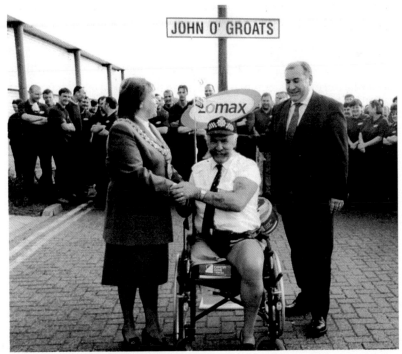

Lady Provost, John Wilmot and Swasie

Finally, after numerous photo calls, interviews and filming, the departure ceremony was formally concluded. Art and I then left Dundee for the day's second lengthy journey, another five-hour drive to Wick where we would be staying for the next three nights. As we left, the Lomax factory workforce waved and cheered us on our way. The whole of Britain would soon be witness to the prowess and quality of such an undoubtedly very impressive and extremely sturdy product.

Tomorrow morning Art and I would then travel from Wick to John O'Groats where we would meet Mr Wilmot and the local police before I would officially 'book out' and commence my lengthy wheelchair push to the (*very*) far distant – Land's End!

The light was fading as Art and I finally arrived at the beautiful little town of Wick in Scotland's far north. We immediately made for the local police station where I introduced ourselves to my police 'colleagues' before going on to our 'hotel'; the local retained fire station. There, we received a great reception from the firefighters who furnished us with a welcome supper to end our, by now very tiresome, day. Our kindly hosts of the Highlands and Islands Fire Brigade at Wick Fire Station then bade us goodnight and in no time Art and I were fast asleep in our sleeping bags on the station floor.

From tomorrow my work would begin in earnest, my *journey of a lifetime* was about to commence!

Chapter Seven
Setting off from 'The Tip'

Day One

AT 6.30 A.M. ON a bright, sunny Friday, 19th of May, I was up and washed before updating my diary in which I meticulously chronicled each day's events. Art was already up and outside checking the van prior to our day's endeavours. I could hear the patter of seagulls as they meandered to and fro across the roof of the single storey building. Alongside Wick Fire Station is a tiny and beautifully picturesque harbour. I savoured the salty smells of the seaside and listened to the continual screams of the gulls as they vied for position to seek anything of gastronomical value that could be found.

Art and I wandered to the local shop for a newspaper and took some pictures of the scene en-route. Eventually, after a hearty, full (English!) breakfast of bacon, eggs, beans and toast, washed down by a large mug of tea, at a local café, Art and I set off for John O'Groats. As we set off the weather changed and the rains came in copious abundance, together with high winds. It looked as if it was going to be a disappointing start, especially for the taking of pictures.

A very wet and windswept scene greeted our 9.30 a.m. arrival at Scotland's famous venue, and due to the inclement weather, there was nobody about as yet. I noticed a small white trailer-van on a car park nearby which displayed a large 'TEAS' sign and had a raised side panel to form a protective canopy. Inside was a no doubt extremely optimistic man *hoping* to sell cups of tea to any brave or hardy tourist who might be courageous enough to brave such elements that prevailed. Art drove our van alongside the trailer where we stopped and purchased two mugs of tea from a very grateful proprietor.

The rain still came down in sheets ably assisted by the wind. This caused the gloomy refreshment vendor to complain bitterly about it being the cause of his acute lack of customers. As I was unable to see a 'John O'Groats' signpost I asked the unhappy vendor if there *was* such a post, as I intended to be photographed alongside it prior to setting off. The man was only too keen to point out that there was such a signpost – *but* – it would not, as yet, have the famous pointer with the words '*Land's End 874 miles*' attached.

The sign would *eventually* appear when – 'the selfish bloody Englishman brings it from his house up the road, later!' hissed the (local) vendor angrily. He went to great pains to inform us that the man was greatly resented by the residents in the locality.

Apparently, he was referring to an immensely unpopular person (an 'immigrant' from over the border!) who, since taking up residence in the area decided to purchase the franchise rights of the post. He then used his position (according to the vendor) to become a greedy, entrepreneurial despot by charging people a fee to be photographed alongside the famous sign. As a matter of principle I decided that I would *certainly* be photographed at the sign for pictorial record, but there was no way I was going to line this man's pocket in order to do so! As we drank our tea, Mr Wilmot and his charming wife Careen then joined Art and I. Mr Wilmot was amazed when he too was told about the sign and the unscrupulous fee seeker.

Thankfully, the inclement weather eventually subsided. The wind and the rain gave way to sunny (but still breezy) spells. Although it remained cold and breezy, at least the light improved and we would be able to get our pictures of the start for posterity – *without* being charged! Eventually, as the tea vendor had prophesised, over the brow of the hill appeared a motorcycle combination, its rider's old leather flying helmet (not a compulsory crash helmet as required by law!) straps flapping in the breeze. It looked like a scenario from a 'Wallace and Grommit' film. The rider made his way to a white post at the cliff top where he parked his combination. He then reached inside the open sidecar and retrieved the '*Land's End 874 miles*' sign, which he promptly secured to the top of the post. The man then retreated to stand in a little sentry box type hut adjacent to 'his' sign. It was at this time that a couple of coaches drew up and disgorged their human cargoes, which comprised mainly of old age pensioners. I saw a number of them approach the sign and stand there as their relatives or friends took photographs. Like a voracious predatory spider, out came 'Septimus' and shot straight to the unsuspecting geriatric 'flies'. He stood there in an intimidating posture, his greedy hand outstretched like an adult Oliver Twist minus his begging bowl.

His efforts to separate the pensioners from their cash proved successful and I saw them hand over their money for the 'privilege' of being pictured at 'his' sign. As I was about to embark on a gruelling, journey of nearly 1000 miles for charity I was determined (*purely* just to be awkward), that I was *not* going to pay one penny, BUT – I *would* be pictured alongside the sign before I set off!

I wheeled my chair up to the sign and shouted to Art and John to snap away. They took a number of pictures as I posed provocatively alongside the sign. Inspector John Grierson and his sergeant from the Thurso police then joined us. The two had kindly attended to see me off and wish me well on my long journey, a kind gesture that I appreciated very much indeed.

When sufficient pictures had been taken (including some with the Police!), Art drew my attention to a number of young wheelchair-bound children who were entering a nearby café with their adult mentors. After calling in at the little Post Office opposite the café to complete the necessary procedure and formalities of my 'registration and booking out' I immediately went over to the café and entered the premises to see the children. I introduced myself to the kids and their accompanying adults. I sat some of them on my knee and we larked about and had our pictures taken before I finally left to begin my mammoth trek.

The cheers of the children and those of their accompanying adults rang in my ears and brought tears to my eyes as I made off from John O'Groats at 10.45 a.m. leaving them (*and the devoid of benevolence*

Swasie alongside signpost at John O'Groats

'*Septimus*') behind. I was experiencing more than the usual amount of pain in my stump lately and today was no exception. This gave me cause for concern as I made my way up the long hills out of John O'Groats as I didn't want anything to prevent the success of this trip. I stopped to pick a bunch of heather from the roadside which I promptly taped to the front of my chair. I intended this to remain with me for the *whole* of the journey 'for luck'.

Police colleagues and Swasie at John O'Groats

A souvenir shop caught my eye as I pushed my chair away from John O'Groats. As I tried to enter I had to negotiate a step. There were a number of expensive glass trinkets as well as china and crockery, which I thought to be 'at risk' being stacked inside, so near the entrance. As I entered I casually remarked, 'I'll *try* and keep the damage down to a minimum'! This remark brought a panicking, instant response from the terrified (male) shopkeeper who was about to either suffer an instant miscarriage or heart attack. Fearful of seeing his treasured china and glass souvenirs destroyed before his very eyes he shrieked, 'No, No – Stay outside – please, *I'll* bring you what you want'! A highly amused Art suddenly appeared and gently pacified the shopkeeper and told me to resume my journey, as he (Art) would get me my souvenirs!

Early Donation; man gives donation leaving John O'Groats

I wandered on along the country roads and I could see the reassuring sight of Art, my backup and 'mentor' in my mirror, five hundred yards behind. As I travelled on, cars stopped regularly and their occupants alighted to put money into my bucket.

Two fully laden coaches passed me then pulled in and stopped ahead. It was the same pensioners that 'Septimus' had previously relieved of some of their cash back at John O' Groats. I was quickly surrounded as they each jostled for position to put their kind donations into my bucket. Much of the cash consisted of notes! The road was temporarily blocked. Traffic travelling in the opposite direction, realising what was going on also came over and gave generously. I was absolutely 'gobsmacked'. I had only travelled a few miles and already I could feel the weight of my laden bucket on the back of my chair.

Another surprise manifested itself shortly after the coaches left. A car travelling to John O'Groats stopped and its two lady and two gentlemen occupants came to me. Each gave a generous donation to my bucket. They informed me that they regularly read my columns in the *Wirral Champion* as they lived in Bebington near to Clatterbridge

Hospital near my home on the Wirral. What a *small* world! My journey to Wick continued during which I was continually stopped by motorists, coaches and householders and handed cash donations ranging from coins to ten and twenty pound bank notes.

Finally, I entered the delightful (and welcome sight of) Wick at 3.10 p.m. having completed my *first* day's trek, the distance being seventeen and a half miles (17.6 to be exact). I was elated, day one had gone very well, and I hadn't experienced any hitches (except for the pain in my stump). Art and I eventually made our way into Wick Fire Station where we were given a fantastic and warm welcome by the retained firefighters and their families. After washing and changing into a clean vest and shorts, (my usual attire) one of the firefighters furnished Art and I with a meal from a nearby Chinese takeaway.

That night there was to be much revelry at Wick station as one of the firefighters was to 'tie the knot' the following day. Festivities started early and in a very short time the 'Very, VERY serious drinking squad' of the Highlands and Islands Fire Brigade – 'Wick Division', captured Art! However, an extremely tired Swasie decided to 'chicken out' (I am teetotal anyway) and I surreptitiously crept outside and into the van where I 'got my head down' and slept the night away.

Day Two

After a refreshing night's sleep, during which I had been completely oblivious to the previous night's festivities, I was woken by a gentle tapping on the van door. It was Art. After he had slept the night away on the station floor (again) he was his usual sprightly self. He had already brewed up and stood there with a mug of hot tea in his hand for me. I quickly 'came to' and gratefully took the hot cuppa from him. I was soon washed and ready for the second day's endeavours and after breakfast at the nearby café all was ready for the arranged arrival of the 'lads'.

Today, I was to have a fire engine escort for five miles as I travelled on to my next destination, Dunbeath nearly 20 miles away. Art, my escort and myself eventually set off at 9.50 a.m. Ten minutes after the start of our journey the fire engine suddenly sped off on a 'shout' into the distance, its two-tone horns blaring and its blue lights flashing. The crew had been directed to a nearby local aerodrome where a fire alarm had been activated. Fortunately, the call was a 'false alarm with good intent' (due to a fault in system) and I was reunited with my escort half an hour later. The machine stayed with me for a further five miles.

During this time the crew, some of whom were walking alongside me and I received many generous donations from motorists, which was brilliant considering we were all way out in the wilderness. Finally the time came for my escort to leave me and return to its base at Wick. We said our goodbyes and I continued on with the reassuring Art in the back-up van two hundred yards behind me as my only escort.

With wick escort on the open road

Swasie and Licensee outside 'Old Smiddy Inn'

We were stopped a couple of miles further on at a little cross roads in the middle of nowhere by the landlady and her son at the 'Old Smiddy Inn', the only building for miles in the vast expanse of heather-clad landscape. The kindly lady put a five-pound note into my bucket and her son handed me a much appreciated cold drink and a bar of chocolate.

Some of the hills I encountered were long and steep but perseverance prevailed and I managed to complete the 'climbs' successfully. I travelled on along the lonely roads and eventually I approached a cottage, again in the middle of nowhere. I saw a lady bending down in front of the cottage as she busily tended the many colourful blooms in her little rockery garden. Suddenly the lady looked up and on seeing me she dashed into the house before returning outside again to wave me to stop. I then recognised the lady as having been one of the adult escorts to the disabled children at the John O'Groats café. She greeted me warmly and handed me a small plastic bag, which was full of one pound coins. 'Here, take this for your cancer charity', she kindly instructed. I thanked her profusely for her more than generous donation and the lady went on to tell me that her eight year old son Daniel was one of the children who had sat on my knee the previous day at John O'Groats. She explained that although Daniel was totally blind and could not talk, he could however hear and understand *everything* that went on about him. 'He *really* enjoyed you having spent some time having fun with him yesterday', said Daniel's mum bringing a lump to my throat. 'Where is he now?' I asked. 'He's in the house', she replied. I asked why she hadn't brought Daniel outside with her to greet me and the lady explained that she thought I wouldn't want to stop too long and interrupt my travels. 'Not at all', I rapidly replied and insisted that she go and bring Daniel outside. She was only too happy to oblige and Daniel and I were quickly and pleasantly reunited once again.

The young boy was wheeled out into the front garden in his wheelchair. I moved alongside him and greeted him, 'Hiya Daniel, it's me Swasie. Do you remember me?' The boy gesticulated with his hands and greeted me in his own warm and friendly way. I placed my arm round him and told him how happy I was to have been able to meet him again. 'What a nice surprise', I said as I ruffled his hair. Again he murmured excitedly and gesticulated with his arms. Daniel's mum leaned over and whispered in my ear, 'You've made him very happy indeed by stopping here today', and went on to add that I had made a 'new friend for life' in her son. I was extremely touched by her comments.

I also deemed it a very honourable privilege to meet someone as wonderful as young Daniel. After spending half an hour with my young friend, during which time the ever present 'David Bailey' in the form of Art Sangster, took a number of photographs of Daniel and I it was, sadly, time to say goodbye.

As I resumed my journey my heart was heavy but I wouldn't have missed that reunion for the world. As I left my new pal I felt a much more humble person, but also a much more rewarded person for

Swasie waves goodbye to Daniel and his Mum

having been in the company of someone so courageous. My own problems were absolutely infinitesimal compared to those of young Daniel. The acute pain in my stump persisted but, after Daniel, this was paled into insignificance and relegated to the 'back boiler'!

Finally, after more lengthy climbs (and descents) I eventually completed the distance to Dunbeath, my bucket having been infinitely enhanced with cash and my life infinitely enhanced by having met Daniel again. Having completed our day's trek, Art and I returned to Wick. Again, all had gone well and I would once again treat myself to an early night. I was receiving calls from Chris (Matron) and my daughter Jo back home keeping me up to date with things. Although the venture was still only in its very early stages, I was happy at the way things were going. Tomorrow I would be making for Helmsdale, another 20-mile push. As this was to be our final night at the beautiful venue of Wick I did venture along with Art to one of the local hostelries to imbibe in a farewell drink (of soda and lime) with the lads of Wick Fire Station. A short time later I left Art and returned back to my 'digs' to get some sleep. I would never forget the lads and their families from Wick, nor their fantastic and warm generosity and hospitality. These same firefighters had given us *three* collection boxes *full of cash*, plus *a cheque for £100*. What truly fantastic people they are. Hopefully, one day I will be able to visit them all once again.

Day Three

After another substantial breakfast at our local harbour café Art and I drove to Dunbeath to resume our journey from where we had left off the day before. It was fascinating to be driven over the distance I had already pushed. This time the stamina-sapping hills seemed very insignificant whilst travelling in the comforts of a motor vehicle. The previous day's 20-mile push to Dunbeath took five and a quarter hours. That journey had consumed a lot of stamina and strength. Today the same journey took a fraction of that time to complete whilst I sat in comfort watching the countryside glide by. Such comfort was short-lived however, and we seemed to have reached Dunbeath almost as soon as we had left Wick!

I was soon underway back on the road resuming my wheelchair trek under my *own* steam. The weather was pleasant and sunny, visibility was good and I was able to admire the stunning views and scenery that prevailed as I devoured yet more mileage in my trusty, arm-powered chariot. I saw wild deer in abundance as they meandered about the acres of heath and heather.

Buzzards circled high overhead as they searched for an opportunity to avail themselves of a tasty meal of rabbit or carrion far below. My arms, shoulders and hands (my brakes) were all in good shape but I was soon sweating in the warm morning air.

One of the biggest tests so far, soon manifested itself in the form of the infamous Berriedale Brae. This was a two-mile descent of 1 : 8 gradient. It was so steep that it was deemed necessary for a gravel pit to be at the base for vehicles to use in an emergency should the gradient prove too much for their brakes. The same *upward* gradient was to greet me when I had to climb up the other side! A lot of people

Swasie descending steep Berriedale Brae

who were aware of this long, steep descent and climb did not think I would manage to negotiate what *most* considered would be an insurmountable obstacle in such a conveyance as mine. Obviously, those who doubted I would successfully complete my journey down the steep hill and on up the other side of this infamous and very steep brae, *failed* to appreciate the amount of dogged inspiration I possessed via my Marje! I shed a large amount of skin during my descent, as my hands were in effect my brakes.

I also lost more fluids than I took aboard via my backpack drink dispenser, the contents of which I rapidly exhausted. Eventually however, after a long and laborious climb up the deep chasm, I finally, and triumphantly, reached the top where Art very quickly furnished me with necessary and generous amounts of cold drinks. I about turned and surveyed all I had 'conquered'! I looked at Scotland's 'Grand Canyon' and exclaimed jubilantly, 'Art, I've *done* it'! My equally jubilant 'Mother Hen' patted me on the back proudly and congratulated me on completing what, he confessed even *he* didn't think, would have been possible. He then confided that the people of Wick thought that Berriedale Brae would not be completed successfully in a wheelchair. Thankfully I had proven them all wrong but I must admit, it *was* a near thing!

After consuming endless amounts of drinks, I resumed my journey and plodded on through the countryside. After the hot sun came the rain, then yet again the welcome sun put in another appearance. It became *very* warm. Eventually the steep gradients gave way to becoming level highways and I made good progress. I was now travelling along lengthy stretches of road across desolate landscapes. Although I admired such a beautiful panorama I felt total isolation. I saw beautiful, long shaggy-haired, wild highland cattle as they meandered and foraged among the desolate acres of the wilderness. I saw Art in my mirror as he alighted from his vehicle to take pictures of the unique, rare and beautiful scenario for posterity. I shouted Marje's name out to the distant horizons as loud as I could, a ritual I was to repeat many times in the highlands. The world about me however remained silent. Utter peace and tranquillity. The only company I enjoyed at this moment were the highland cattle, some red deer and the ever-present buzzards as they constantly circled overhead, *and* of course my constant companion, Art. My 'mentor', whom I could see in my mirror, was a little white dot in the distance as he continually monitored and oversaw my progress.

It certainly was, without doubt, a 'God's little acre' that I was travelling through. I slogged on and on making my way towards Helmsdale, now and again passing little starched white-thatched or peat-roofed cottages, many of which were derelict and their occupants long gone. I was truly fascinated by these little buildings. Oh! What stories they could tell! I saw numerous stone-built bridges under which flowed tinkling little streams. I was sorely tempted to stop and drink from those tempting waters. The whole area was nothing short of an artist's dream.

Swasie at the top of the Brae after successful completion

I finally reached Helmsdale, and completed the day's push of 19 miles at 4.30 p.m. This now brought my total miles completed so far to over 50! Art and I made our way on to Dornoch Fire Station. This was to be our new 'home' for the next two nights. As we entered the quiet picturesque little village of Dornoch (which was to receive worldwide publicity and fame some time later when the millionaire singer and mega star Madonna was married to film mogul Guy Ritchie at the little village church) we were directed to the fire station by a local police constable. Again, being a retained fire station (the *whole* of the Highlands and Islands Fire Brigade consists of retained personnel only), Art had to telephone ahead to the station commander's house and inform him of our estimated time of arrival (ETA). On arrival we were met by the station's Sub Officer who then introduced us to the rest of his crew. As was to be the norm throughout our entire journey, *nothing* was too much trouble for our firefighting hosts. After a wash and brush up we were directed to a local hotel, the Eagle, where arrangements had already been made for us to partake in a substantial and most enjoyable evening meal.

At the conclusion of our meal and after a few refreshing drinks, Art and I made our weary way back to the station to avail ourselves of an early night and a good night's sleep. Our peaceful slumbers were shattered during the night however when the 'bells went down' (the crew were turned out to an incident in the early hours). This was to happen many, many times during the ensuing weeks!

Day Four

I woke up to the sound of birds singing, and surprisingly, the squeals of gulls. It was a bright, sunny morning. The day looked as if it promised to be warm and dry. After the short trek to the Eagle hotel for a hearty breakfast Art and I returned to Helmsdale to resume my 20-mile push from there to Dornoch. Traffic was heavier than I had so far experienced at first, but the roads became quiet as my journey and the morning wore on. After a few miles I approached the historic and picturesque Dunrobin Castle. As I made my way along, I saw a hiker clad in waterproofs and bearing a rucksack, walking the lonely road towards me. We both stopped to greet each other and introduce ourselves. The hiker was a pleasant young lady, Pinky McKay. Pinky informed me that she had almost completed *her* journey from Land's End to John O'Groats, having set out on her momentous walk 44 long, arduous and tiresome days earlier. I turned and looked back and saw the faithful Art as he dismounted from his vehicle.

As usual, Art would again record *this* occasion in his skilled photographer's pictorial form. During our brief conversation Pinky and I promised to keep in touch, and update each other as to our individual progress. Pinky, like myself had lost her loved one to the dreaded scourge of cancer, and again like me, had decided to do something about it by assisting the fight to eradicate this merciless killer amongst us. As a result of that casual meeting on that warm, sunny morning in the Scottish countryside, Pinky and I formed a warm and lasting friendship.

After a short while we bade each other goodbye and each resumed our journey. As Art and I passed through the village of Golspie later,

Swasie meets Pinky McKay

Art spotted a bank and decided to stop and bank the monies we had raised so far. Although this was only day four, the amount so far received via the many kind roadside donors, had amounted to nearly £400. Considering the desolate and barren countryside we had so far trekked through, this was an amazing amount to have raised. This shows the true generosity and benevolence of the Scottish people. What an incentive to ensure my perseverance. I left Art at the bank and continued on. Local villagers and shopkeepers constantly stopped me in my tracks to donate generously to my bucket. Some bought copies of my books *Wheelchair Pilot* and *Off the Cuff* (my autobiography), the profits from both also going into my bucket. By the time Art left the bank to continue his pursuit of me, I had travelled only a matter of a couple of hundred yards!

Time (and the day) marched on. I was pleasantly surprised when my colleague (and tutor) at Radio Clatterbridge, Vic Charles, rang me to conduct a live interview on air. Shortly after this I was privileged to receive a similar call from the well-known and extremely popular Radio Merseyside presenter, Linda McDermott. Linda too conducted an interview live on air to the people of Merseyside while Art and I passed through more beautifully quaint villages as our journey progressed.

Finally, at the welcome conclusion to yet another successful day, my 20-mile journey to Dornoch was over. As I entered the village I called at the police station to meet police colleagues. The Inspector purchased a copy of *Wheelchair Pilot* and Art and I had a welcome cuppa with the rest of the section before returning to the fire station. On arriving there, I was greeted there by a press photographer from the *Northern Times*. He took a picture to illustrate an article in the forthcoming edition regarding my 'venture'. When he had left us we were again to sample the gastronomically appetising fayre at the Eagle Hotel before retiring to our sleeping bags for the night. This time our night's slumbers were *not* to be interrupted by a 'shout' during the night!

Day Five

Up at 6.40 a.m. to a bright sunny morning after being woken by Art, who promptly handed me a welcome and much appreciated hot mug of tea. What an utter privilege to have someone as good as Art to look after me!

Today we would be leaving our 'digs' at Dornoch to head for far off Invergordon 24 miles away. Tonight we would be sleeping at the Brigade's area training school. Again we fuelled up on a full breakfast at the Eagle before setting off at 8.30 a.m. By now the sky had clouded over and it looked like I was in for a soaking.

As I was leaving Dornoch I was stopped by a motorist and the lady driver gave me a twenty-pound note. On leaving her I then passed the local school and was greeted by tumultuous cheers as the pupils lined the railings and school balcony waving me on. Those two little 'send offs' by the lady and the pupils more than compensated for the dark and threatening skies above me. The rain was not long in arriving, *with a vengeance*. The rain came down in a torrential downpour. In no time at all I was soaked through to the skin. As if that wasn't bad enough, along came a powerful (head) wind just to add to the meteorological cocktail. Oh! How delighted I became! I made my way over the Dornoch Bridge where I was well and truly open to the elements and blasted by a freezing wind coming in across the equally freezing water. Passing vehicles drenched me in heavy spray, especially the big trucks. As I crossed the bridge, rain or no rain, it didn't eliminate the generosity of a kindly lady motorist who took the trouble to brave the elements by stopping and getting out of her vehicle to hand me a ten pound note. The lady's acute generosity furnished her with an almighty soaking before she could get back into the warm confines of her car.

Such benevolence makes me feel so utterly humble. Mile after mile I continued to slog as the rain came down in sheets. A short distance further on, still on the bridge, three cyclists travelling in the opposite direction came over and each deposited their cash into the

Lady donates to Swasie on Dornoch Bridge in heavy rain

bucket. They, like the lady I met on day four, were en-route to John O'Groats from Land's End – *to raise money for their own charity*! Again, this highlights the complete and selfless generosity of those who care for others.

Eventually the sky started to clear and the rain gradually eased off and stopped. As I pushed on, vehicles swished by, enveloping me in their fine spray. Suddenly a car pulled into the side ahead of me and stopped. The male driver and his female passenger then got out of the vehicle and made their way back to me. I couldn't believe my eyes when I recognised the driver. He was none other than my ex-Inspector at Wallasey, 400 miles away: Inspector Cooper 'Cooperman' my old boss and his wife! They were both equally as shocked as I was. It transpired that on his subsequent retirement from the police, Mr Cooper and his wife moved from the Wirral to the upper reaches of Scotland where they had settled to enjoy a life of highland tranquillity. What a shock for 'Cooperman' when that tranquillity was shattered on his seeing me – again! I bet he too reached for his valium!

Even though the weather was 'iffy' and it was a long journey today, I made a slight detour to pass through Tain. Although it was a small town, it was nevertheless a busy little venue. My detour paid off and I received many donations from the kindly population as I passed through. Back on the open road, I was 'beaten up' by a low flying Tornado aircraft as it exercised over and alongside the nearby shoreline.

After many steep and long climbs, twists and bends, my tiring and lengthy day's trek eventually landed me at Invergordon. This is a very pleasant 'resort' town on the shores of the Cromarty Firth. We arrived at the fire station and again Art and I were given warm welcome and adequately fed by the generous wife of the station commander. My wet clothes were taken and placed into the warm confines of the station drying room. A wash and a change later and I felt brand new again. The Station Officer's sister kindly brought in a bed *and* a mattress for *me* to sleep on but poor Art had to make do with his sleeping bag on a camp bed!

That evening, I was asked to address a group of 'Rainbows' from the local Brownie pack. It was my pleasure to do so. At the conclusion of my talk, the children asked for my autograph. Many insisted that I autograph their yellow uniform jerseys with my black pen, no doubt to the delight of their mothers! Suddenly I was elevated to 'celebrity status'! Their adult leaders, Brown Owl and her two colleagues,

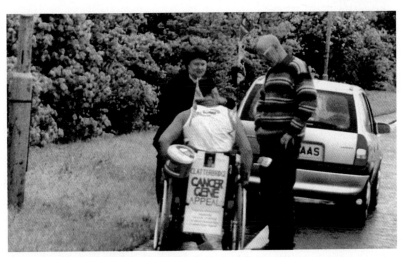

Swasie meets 'Cooperman' and his wife

Signing Brownies shirts at Invergordon fire station

donated generously to my bucket. They also purchased a copy of *'Wheelchair Pilot'* for their headquarter's 'library'. Even though it was now 'after hours', Art and I were taken to the nearby Dounmore Whisky distillery for a conducted tour. There, Art and I were each presented with a bottle of the 'hard stuff' – and me being a non-drinker! On our return to the station, the firefighters donated £50 to my charities. This brought my last two day's 'donations' to £260.74 and in turn brought the trip's cash collections for the past five days to a total of £608.31. This offered much encouragement that generated a burning incentive to successfully complete the mega mileage involved in this venture.

The day finally drew to a close and an extremely tired wheelchair crusader turned into bed and crashed out, even though Art and I were allocated the station's lecture room as our dormitory. No sooner had my head hit the pillow than I was immediately overcome by the anaesthesia of slumbering enchantment.

Day Six

Art and I were up at 5.00 a.m. and as I wrote a comprehensive entry into the station's incident memo book thanking profusely our generous hosts at Invergordon Fire Station, Art busied himself with another major task; that of facilitating the morning brew! I retrieved my by now warm and completely dry clothing and placed it into my bag. Today we were off to Drumnadrochit, another lengthy (27 miles) slog. Yesterday's rain had softened my hands and caused one or two blisters and cracks to appear. I dabbed them with surgical spirit as this hardens the skin, although the price to pay for this 'cure' is its powerful sting, which lasts for some time, however, the eventual result is well worth such a painful effort. After a couple more mugs of tea were consumed, Art and I hit the road at 8.30 a.m. and 'set course' for our distant venue.

After travelling a short distance, I noticed that my mileometer was not registering. This gave me cause for concern, as I needed to monitor my progress, mile by mile. Although Art was keeping a meticulous record of every yard travelled, I needed to be in control of keeping check on the distance and time I was 'under power'. We were on busy main roads now and the traffic was building up.

Soon we were amongst the morning peak hour traffic heading into Inverness. Although the sight of Art's white van in my mirror reassured me, I was a little apprehensive as the volume of heavy traffic was increasing. More intimidating was the sheer speed at which some impatient motorists were travelling. Eventually we approached the bridge, which crossed the Firth of Inverness and led into the busy and congested town. I looked into my mirror and was pleased to see that we had a police escort. The police car was behind Art with its blue light flashing. I was pleased, and thankful, to see that the police had kindly provided us with an escort during this particularly dangerous stage of our journey into Inverness. Just then my chairborne mobile phone rang. It was Art! 'Swas, when you get to the other side of the Firth, the police want you to pull into the lay-by just past the end of the bridge', instructed my mentor. I acknowledged Art's call and after running the gauntlet of the heavy traffic and successfully crossing the bridge I pulled in as instructed. Art pulled in and the police car drew alongside us.

I introduced Art and myself to the police officer and the constable then informed us that he had been sent to intercept a man in a wheelchair, loose on the extremely busy A9 into Inverness. The officer went on to explain that numerous motorists had rang the police worrying at the thought that someone had 'escaped' from a nursing home and was running amok amongst the early morning rush hour traffic! Art explained all, emphasising the fact that our endeavours had been faxed to ALL Fire Brigades and Police Forces throughout the whole of our intended route during the preceding months. The sympathetic and friendly police officer introduced himself as Kevin and cordially invited us to allow him to escort us to Inverness Police Station where we could meet his colleagues. Kevin's kind offer was gratefully accepted and he led the way for the next mile, through the busy town to his station. Kevin ushered Art and me into the station's 'inner sanctum' and in no time we found ourselves up via the lift on the first floor in the officers' dining room.

The Inverness Area Commander, Superintendent Gary Sutherland then entered the room with two Chief Inspector colleagues. Tea and biscuits were soon provided and we all enjoyed a convivial get together. Gary eventually remembered having received the previous faxes relating to our 'intrusion' onto his busy patch. His admission generated much banter, especially from his subordinate constable who had been sent to intercept the 'geriatric escapee in a wheelchair on the busy A9!' The police went on to say how much they were impressed by the professional standards of safety that had been instigated by Lomax concerning the venture.

The large lettered rear-warning board and its flashing strobe lights certainly impressed all present that nothing had been spared to ensure safety prevailed (the senior officers had previously taken the trouble to go outside and inspect our vehicle). On learning of my faulty mileometer, Superintendent Sutherland informed me that they (the Inverness police) enjoyed a good relationship with the nearby Halfords cycle stores. He requested his constable (Kevin) to take me there to see if my faulty piece of equipment could be

Halfords repair Swasie's mileometer

rectified. The extremely obliging management, in the form of Mr Brian Aitkin and his equally obliging assistant David Ross, not only repaired my faulty instrument, but they also generously supplied me with a spare and furnished me with £70 worth of equipment for use during my trip. I am more than grateful for the kindness of the Halfords' staff at Inverness.

A fully replenished Art and I, and our van, eventually and reluctantly, left our kind police and civilian benefactors, and continued our journey. The long climb out of Inverness wasn't easy. I pushed on towards Fort William and reached the Caledonian Canal. As I made my way south towards the still very distant England, I crossed over another bridge and on towards Loch Ness. Workmen were busily engaged with roadworks and as I passed them, each of the men left what they were doing and crossed over to donate generously to my bucket. I felt as though I was really making headway through Scotland now, although there was a long, long way to go before I would enter England and close the kilted gate behind me!

The rain started again and although it wasn't heavy, it was however persistent (and cold). I was then contacted by the Moray FM Radio chat show and interviewed live on air via my mobile phone. The rain eventually stopped, but not until I was soaked through yet again! Loch Ness finally came into view. The loch is 32 miles long but after a short distance along its bank I completed my day's (mainly wet) journey of 23 miles. Today, I had completed my first one hundred miles!

I would continue my trek from the same venue in the morning. I was by now soaking wet and looking forward to the warm confines of Inverness Fire Station and tucking in to the evening meal with the lads in the canteen. Before this could happen however, I was met at the station and interviewed by the local press, the Inverness Courier who would publish a feature and picture in their paper two days later (Friday, 26th May). I was rapidly beginning to feel that I was actually back in the brigade myself!

It was now the absolute norm to be furnished with copious amounts of warm and generous hospitality by our truly professional fire service 'colleagues'. As at every station, we were again fed and watered and given privileged sleeping accommodation. Art and I were billeted in the LF's (Leading Firefighters') room.

This *was* sheer luxury! Immediately after tea I met the station's senior officer (the DO) then retired to 'my' room to get a good night's sleep. Art was, once again, captured by one of the lads, namely the station's 'Ben Fund' rep, and *forcibly* taken on a tour of the town's hostelries!

Day Seven

Up at 7.30 a.m. I was allowed the additional 'privilege' of washing and getting ready in the Station Officer's wash room. This afforded the privacy I needed as, being unable to use a shower, I have to sit at an ordinary wash bowl, naked, to wash and dress – not a particularly enjoyable ritual in front of all and sundry! After a spruce up, Art and I packed our things and made for the canteen for a cup of tea with the night watch, prior to them going off duty. There was a fair wind today with rain showers. It looked as though I was in for another soaking! Eventually Art and I made off to resume today's trek from where we finished yesterday at Drumnadrochit.

However, breakfast called first! We stopped at a little café approximately a mile before our starting point. There, we enjoyed the culinary delights of the establishment's proprietor who was also the chef. He furnished Lomax's hungry duo with a large plate of bacon, egg, beans and toast, accompanied by the traditional mug of hot tea. As we sat at the table a number of workmen customers sitting nearby asked us where we were from and what we were up to. Art proudly explained all and impressed everyone present. As Art went on, everyone, including the café owner, delved into their pockets before donating readily and generously to our bucket. Soon after, Art and I rose from our table, our hunger satisfied. As we left, all present offered their encouragement and sincere best wishes. Some of the customers (who were workers engaged in resurfacing the road outside) summoned their colleagues already at work nearby and encouraged them to add to our coffers. Again, more cash was generously donated.

I resumed my push down the side of the famous Loch Ness and progressed steadily onwards. The wind whipped up the loch's waters and large 'white horses' appeared on the surface, making it very 'lumpy' for a number of boats that were negotiating the chilly waters. Large black clouds then deposited a heavy squall completely obliterating the distant far end of the loch. It now appeared as though I was looking out to sea as all land was erased during the downpour and this created a false horizon. The squall soon reached me and I was dripping wet within seconds. Although it was only 11.00 a.m., the light was so poor, it was necessary for me to switch on all the lights on my chair to ensure maximum visibility. Art rang me from the van a short distance behind to verify that my six rear, red flashing lights *and* my blue, flashing strobe, were all bright and working correctly to ensure my safety. I silently thanked Duracell for making such powerful and reliable long life batteries. I also had three powerful little white lights on the front of my chair. *All* my lights (with the exception of my blue strobe 'torch') were 'Cat Eye' cycle lamps. Having previously tried *numerous* well-known makes of batteries during my many 'nocturnal' journeys, there were none that could match the duration and strength of Duracell. Their dynamic little packs of power I now *unhesitatingly* and totally recommend to all. Art went on to confirm the importance of my 'illuminations', as these were the only indication to him of my presence during that heavy downpour.

Thankfully the unwelcome and almost obliterating shower eventually exhausted itself and the black clouds turned grey before they finally gave way to sunny spells. I was left a drenched, cold and soggy bundle, my handlebar moustache drooping to make me look like a walrus that had just come out of the water. I was pushing alongside the famous loch and had to negotiate many unpleasant steep and twisting hills.

Back on the straight and level I pushed on in the by now, thankfully warm sunshine. I started to hear the faint, lamenting wail of bagpipes playing in the distance. This seemed to enhance and authenticate the beautiful Scottish scenery I was travelling through. I eventually approached the source of the 'Highland Lament'. As I neared a lay-by I saw, to my amazement, the magnificent figure of an extremely smart and handsome tartan clad Highland piper. His kilted, uniformed attire was immaculate. What a striking figure he was. Gathered about him were a number of people, one of whom was a young boy in a wheelchair. I just *had* to stop and savour this beautiful scenario. The curious piper, on seeing the unusual sight of a vest and shorts clad middle-aged man in an ordinary wheelchair bedecked with colourful pennants, enquired what it was I was undertaking. On

Piper Murdo and Swasie alongside Loch Ness

being told, the generous piper, Mr Murdo Urquhart (himself an ex-Scottish Police Officer) immediately went to a nearby table on which stood a little collection box. This box contained donations from people (tourists) who had been entertained by Murdo's excellent roadside Scottish renditions via his bagpipes. Without hesitation, the generous piper dipped into his box and gave me £5 for my bucket. I reciprocated his kindness by personally endorsing a copy of *Wheelchair Pilot*, which Art had produced from the van. On seeing this, the parents of the boy in the wheelchair then insisted on purchasing a copy for their son, which I duly signed. The family were tourists from Australia and they too were savouring the scenic delights of Scotland before they were to return back 'down under' in a few days time. Eventually, curiosity got the better of the lady from the outback! She turned to the piper and candidly asked, 'Doun' moind me aaskin' sport, bit is it true what they say about a Scotsman having nothing under his kilt?' No doubt having been asked this laboriously boring question a thousand times before, Murdo's instant, but polite, reply was, 'Aye, it's true, there's nae't there, just two bombers an' a spitfire!' The lady's inquisitive curiosity was satisfied and she giggled at such a thought.

At the conclusion of our jovial *and unforgettable* meeting, I moved on. I resumed my trek towards my next night's stay at far away Fort Augustus as Murdo resumed his roadside piped renditions. Moving further down alongside the famous loch, Art then instructed me to stop at a venue where he would take some pictures. I duly obliged and Art took some pictures of me with the 'Loch Ness Monster' behind me.

The 'monster' was in fact a tourist attraction on the side of a large pond in the grounds of a hotel. After our little 'photo shoot' we moved on again to burn more tread from the tyres of my wheels and casters.

Eventually the day's hard slog ended at 3.45 p.m. as I pushed my way into Fort Augustus (where I was bitten by an Alsatian dog!). I first made for the police station for a quick cuppa with the Bobbies before moving on to the fire station where yet another wonderful 'fire service' welcome awaited Art and I. Wives of the station's firefighters furnished sandwiches as well as tea and coffee. They also took the trouble to bring two beds into the station for us. On arrival however, the *first* thing I would have to do would be to make for the nearest 'sink' for my ritual wash and brush up as well as cleaning my bite wound with antiseptic! This done, I returned a short time later washed and dressed in warm, dry clothing. *Now* I could settle down to enjoy the wonderful spread that was laid before me.

Tonight, it was to be the Brigade's weekly training night so Art and I made ourselves scarce and ventured along to a local pub for an evening meal. We eventually returned to the station after the conclusion of the lads' training session and after an hour's chatting with them, the 'troops' finally dispersed. I made a cup of tea as Art completed the daily 'log' before we counted and bagged the day's cash donations. After these tasks were concluded the pair of us then retired to our beds. Again, as on previous occasions, our slumbers were interrupted by two 'shouts' during the night. This, however, was always to be *par* for the course. Indeed, this was a small price to pay for the warm and generous hospitality that we would enjoy during the *whole* of our lengthy trek!

Day Eight

After rising at 7.00 a.m. Art and I were greeted by Chris, one of the firefighters. Unknown to Art and I, Chris and his charming wife owned a large hotel nearby, the very upmarket 'Caledonian Hotel'. The hotel was the venue for the majority of both British and foreign holidaymakers and was nearly always full to capacity. Chris insisted that Art and I have a hearty breakfast at his hotel, courtesy of him and his wife. We both gratefully accepted and despite our insistence to pay for our substantial meals, the generous couple would not hear of it. As well as Chris and his brigade colleagues donating generously to our 'bucket' at the station, our hotel hosts gave a further cash donation. This typified the benevolence we were to encounter all the way down the country. I left the warm confines of Chris's Caledonian Hotel and pushed my way out of Fort Augustus (and away from aggressive Alsatians) for a final photo shoot with the town's fire crew and their machine down at the loch side.

This completed, the rains came again. I pushed myself up and out of the town and headed for Fort William where we would be staying for the next two nights.

Our journey to Fort William involved many arduous long and steep hill climbs. The hills never seemed to end. As I made my weary way along, a group of cyclists were gathered near a van on the opposite side of the road as they consumed cold drinks. Just then a voice shouted, 'Bloody hell, it's Swasie!' I was then invited over to join the throng where I was also given a cool, refreshing drink of orange juice. The cyclists were members of the 'Wirral Autism Society' from near my home in Wirral. They were making their way to John O'Groats from Land's End to generate money for their charity. Even so, it didn't stop each and every one of them contributing to *my* charity! Their kind gesture was much appreciated by myself and Art who, as usual, ensured he obtained a pictorial record of our meeting. What a small world it seemed to be!

Our journey continued on as the ever persistent rain returned. The rain continued for the rest of the day's trek and a very wet and not too warm (and not too happy) wheelchair pilot eventually reached Fort William at 4.00 p.m. I had been pushing for six hours. As usual, we made for the confines of the local police station where we were greeted by a stony faced young sergeant. Although he knew who we were and what we were doing, he made Art and I as feel as welcome as a cat in a birdcage. He asked us what we wanted. I told him that I had called in to say hello to my 'colleagues'. 'Okay, so you've called and said hello, now what?' he asked in a most unfriendly manner. I told him we were 'doing the end-to-end' and we were wet and cold. His cold reply was to inform us that 'We have end-to-enders coming through here every week'. By this time I began to

Fort William

suffer an acute sense of humour loss. 'Oh, so you're inundated with legless police sergeants whizzing through town in wheelchairs all the time are you?' I retorted. I asked the inhospitable enhancer of police and public relations if the station had a canteen. 'No', he replied before telling us that he was busy and 'would there be anything else?' 'No, there bloody wouldn't', I snapped as I spun my chair round and left.

Art and I then wearily made our way to Fort William Fire Station to spend the night in our sleeping bags on the snooker room floor. We shared the 'floor' with two West Midlands firefighters who were also passing through during their own charity 'Coast to Coast' cycle ride. There wasn't a place to dry my wet clothes, as there was no heat in the building. Although the old building had numerous radiators, these were all cold!

Day Nine

After a very restless and mainly sleepless night I finally rose for the day's toils at 7.00 a.m. to yet another morning of drizzle. I was stiff and ached all over. The station floor was very hard indeed. Today, breakfast consisted of some biscuits and a couple of mugs of tea.

I set off in the morning rain but I found the view and the coastline exhilarating as I pushed on to Glencoe and the Scottish Highlands. After I had travelled a few miles the two West Midlands firefighters caught up with me and stopped to put some money into my bucket. They then made off and disappeared into the distance as I plodded on yet again. Although there were a number of hills, some quite 'naughty', my trip to Glencoe was perfect and uneventful. The sun eventually came out and the day warmed up. Although the roads were not very busy, there were however, a number of motorists that stopped to 'feed' my ever-hungry bucket.

As I passed the beautifully picturesque village of Ballachulish on the shores of Loch Leven, I couldn't resist stopping at a beautiful miniature stone church surrounded by a mass of bluebells. These

Bluebells and little church in Ballachulish

were the favourite flowers of both Marje and myself so I picked one of them to place onto today's page in my diary where it would remain. I asked Art to photograph the beautiful scene. I needn't have bothered, he had already done so!

Half a mile further on and I arrived at the equally beautiful village of Glencoe which snuggled peacefully on the side of the loch at the base of the mountains under the lee of the famous and much photographed 'Three Sisters'. The place was nothing short of a little paradise. Little fishing boats of many colours bobbed about on the blue waters of the loch. Behind these were little islands, some which were the final resting place of long departed crofters and highlanders. As Art and I were now rather peckish we entered the little village to seek out a restaurant or café. We soon came across a large sign bearing the words 'Mrs Matheson's Tea-room and Restaurant'. On entering the meticulously clean little establishment, Art and I were warmly greeted by the lady herself. The lady, on seeing all the pennants on my chair, keenly enquired as to what we were about. Art and I were soon tucking into a piping hot lunch of potatoes, venison and vegetables with copious amounts of tea. The

Looking down on Loch Leven from Pap of Glencoe

nearby patrons, on hearing of our endeavours, kindly contributed to my bucket, as did Mrs Matheson and her staff. The lady would not hear of charging us for our meal and insisted on it being 'with the compliments of the house'. It was now 1.00 p.m. and having completed just over 20 miles, it was here I would finish for the day and resume from here the following morning.

Art and I returned to Fort William and this time we were warmly invited to the police station by the lady on the reception desk who knew who I was (she and her colleagues at Fort William are regular readers of my column in *Police News*). On our arrival Art and I were ushered through to the (non-existent!) canteen by Willie Muir, a very friendly middle-aged sergeant of lengthy service.

Art and I were then surprised when Willie, our kindly sergeant host, informed us that there were some ladies at the counter who wished to join us. The 'ladies' were brought through and we were pleasantly surprised to find it was Sarah the Director from Lomax with her young daughter and her friend.

That night Sarah treated Art and I to a wonderful dinner at the posh Onich Hotel. We enjoyed a most wonderful evening, courtesy of the kind and benevolent Sarah. Eventually Art and I, after enjoying the gastronomic delights of the evening, bade farewell to our two charming and benevolent lady hostesses and retreated back to Fort William Fire Station to our 'floor' for the night.

Day Ten

At 8.45 a.m. I started the day's push from the beautiful little village of Glencoe. It was a hell of a climb out of the village up into the cold and unforgiving highlands. I would have a long, hard slog ahead of me today! First, I had to climb up and out of the village, which in itself was no easy task as the long, steep gradients were horrendously punishing. My distant destination today was a long and strenuous 28 miles away. It would be a long haul, which I anticipated would take at least nine or ten hours, before I would arrive at the village of Crianlaroch, when I could then take advantage of my overnight sanctuary at the local youth hostel. My day started cool but dry and bright. As I left the sleepy village and made my way past the last of the cottages, I witnessed a truly rare sight. A cheeky little pine marten pricked his head up and eyed me suspiciously from the confines of a neat little cottage garden. The audacious little animal then darted from the flower bordered little haven into an adjacent little copse of

Pine Marten

Looking down to Jimmy Saville's cottage, Glencoe

trees after rummaging amongst the abandoned contents of a dog's feeding bowl near the cottage door.

Traffic was almost none existent as I struggled, grunted and sweated my way up the steep, long and winding hills out of Glencoe. Onwards I pushed, passing the beautiful little cottage where I stopped to deliver a copy of my book *Wheelchair Pilot* to its resident and owner, Sir Jimmy Saville.

I pressed on and up towards the 'White Corries', where the well-known ski resort sits among the snow-capped peaks. I continued to sweat, even though the sleet and rain paid me yet another unwelcome visit as I pushed on and struggled 'skywards'! The droning rattle of my back-up vehicle's diesel engine faded into a slight hum before eventually all became quiet. Art had now dropped well behind to give me maximum protection by warning any motorists via his large sign with flashing lights on the rear of his van that a slow moving wheelchair's presence was ahead. The only sounds now were my own grunts and gasps as I continued my laborious ascent into the inhospitable mountains.

It was here, in this very area, on 13th February 1692, that a horrendous massacre of men, women and children took place.

Robert Campbell of Glen Lyon and his men accepted the traditional Scottish hospitality from the elderly clan chief Ian McDonald, his wife, and fellow clansmen and their families. Then, in the dead of that fateful 13th night of February just over 400 years ago, Campbell and his soldiers abused their hosts' hospitality in a way never to be forgotten. Campbell and his men massacred most of their friendly hosts, including the chief and his wife with whom they had earlier been playing cards. Not even women or children were spared. Campbell razed the McDonalds' huts and cottages to the ground then made off with their flocks, herds and ponies. Those who managed to escape into the surrounding hills were to freeze to death in the appalling wintry conditions that prevailed. This never to be forgotten act of shame and disgrace has caused the area to be hence known as, 'The Glen of Weeping'. There exists to this day, a monument to the McDonalds who were to die due to such treachery. The area has an eerie silence and it is said that this is due to the presence of the spirits of those who perished. Even to this day there still exists a mild form of 'animosity' between some Campbells and McDonalds!

On and on I climbed. Other than my grunts, total silence prevailed. I felt as though my arms and shoulders would burst at my strenuous efforts to power my way ever upwards. I repeatedly shouted my Marje's name at the top of my voice and tears flowed down my cheeks as my beloved wife and sweetheart's name echoed back to me from the towering snow-capped peaks that surrounded me.

Distant snow caps

Golden Eagle

It was here that I witnessed nature in the raw! I saw a magnificent Golden Eagle plummet from the skies to snatch a complacent rabbit in its razor sharp talons before soaring away with its prey.

The big bird gave a shrill like yelp as though announcing its kill as its powerful wings lifted it up and away. What a cruel but truly magnificent and fascinating spectacle to have witnessed. Eventually I was relieved (and grateful) when the steep, narrow road finally levelled out to give me some respite. Up to now the weather had been reasonably kind on occasions. However, as I pushed on past the Corries Ski Resort the skies blackened and within minutes I was in the midst of a freezing cold downpour.

The elements had decided to anoint my vest and shorts clad frame with copious amounts of rain and sleet to mingle with my perspiration. I now needed the added protection of the cycle lamps fitted to the front and rear of my chair. Eventually the weather improved and the skies cleared again. A car swished by giving me a further soaking as it drove through puddles left by the rain. Oh dear, this did absolute wonders for my sapping morale! The car stopped ahead of me. The lady driver got out to congratulate me on having successfully negotiated the steep climbs out of Glencoe. The lady was none other than my kind and generous benefactor of yesterday, Mrs Matherson from the Glencoe Tea Room. She gave me a warm and gentle hug, wished me well and handed me yet another donation before vanishing off in a cloud of spray, leaving me alone once more to battle the elements. I was soaked to the skin (yet again) and pushed on relentlessly through the highlands and over Ranoch Mor, eventually passing through Tyndrum. As I made on towards my goal, now five miles away, at Clianlaroch, I saw a large, beautifully majestic red stag.

Red Stag on the heather at Clianlaroch

Swasie meets a 'Jacobite' Neil Munroe

He stood motionless and aloof, his magnificent antlers held high as he surveyed all before him. His two front legs were strategically placed on an outcrop of rock. The wonderful beast looked so dignified and elegant. This was the *real* Scotland and I felt privileged to be intruding into the domain of such beautiful wildlife. To 'authenticate' things further, just as I reached the top of another steep climb I heard someone yell in a broad Scottish brogue, 'C'mere yer bastard, I wanna gi' yer a big hug'!

I just could *not* believe what I saw! For some time Art had been taking the Mickey out of me saying that wild highlanders with big claymors would accost me once I entered the highlands. Here, now, for all to see was just that! Out of the fir trees at the side of the road appeared a scruffy looking 'Jacobite' Highland clansman. He stood there in full highland regalia brandishing a long wicked looking (authentic) claymor. Surely this must be a windup I thought. However, Art also could not believe what he was seeing. All his japes and imaginative 'warnings' had suddenly come to fruition! The sight of this man was fearsome. His long vivid and unruly red hair and beard would scare the living daylights out of anyone. All I could say to his request for a hug was, 'Feel free mate, help yourself', as I had no intention of denying him the pleasure of his 'hug'!

Art drew up behind me and stopped. In no time he was out with his camera, recording for posterity this unique occasion. Art took numerous photographs of this unbelievable spectacle, the sight of a kilted warrior hugging his wheelchair prodigy!

In actual fact, the 'Jacobite' was a Mr Neil Munroe, who himself was on a 'Mission', a 'Crusade'. He was sleeping rough as he travelled on foot from Banochburn to Ben Nevis to raise funds to assist in the fight to stop the sale of parts of Ben Nevis. Neil had heard about my trek and made a point of intercepting me on my travels. After (many more) pictures were taken and Neil and I exchanged particulars, we each resumed our respective journeys. It was certainly a privilege and an experience to have met such a wonderful fellow.

Eventually I finally reached Clianlaroch to complete my day's hard and extremely eventful toil. Even though traffic had been sparse, Art and I had received a few extremely generous donations during the day's trek. After a hot bath and a hearty meal at our overnight 'digs', I finally made for my bed to crash out and savour a night's welcome slumbers.

Chapter Eight
A Senior Rank Joins the Escort as we Head South

Day Eleven

AFTER A RESTFUL night I rose to wash and prepare for the day's onward push South. Art and I called at a little café in the village for breakfast prior to our start. Fully fed and watered, I set off from Clianlaroch wondering if the weather would be kind today. My trusty escort, Art, followed at a discreet and safe distance behind ensuring my safety with his sign and flashing lights. As I had slept peacefully the previous night, Art had busied himself counting and bagging the donations. These now totalled over £1,000. Banking facilities had already been arranged via Lomax to enable Art to deposit cash into our charity account as we travelled.

Once out into the sticks, again the beautiful scenery unfolded. I hoped there was not going to be any rain (or hills) today. With my mobile phone fully charged and strapped to my chair I awaited anticipated calls from the media, John Wilmot of Lomax, son Ron, daughter Jo and of course Chris, my 'mentor' back home. After many miles of hard slogging, but perfect views of beautiful country, I came to a long, two-mile downhill stretch. The road was narrow and very steep. As I started my long descent, I had to hold my wheels tightly to maintain a steady, slow descent. I saw a large black car parked in a lay-by with a blue strobe light flashing on its roof. I thought, 'Great, I've got a police escort for a change!' As I approached the vehicle the driver opened his door and got out to greet me. I saw his white shirt with three 'pips' on his shoulder. I thought he was a Chief Inspector from the Local Police Force.

Long, lonely road and Lochside cottage

However, as I drew near to him I saw that the 'pips' on his shoulder were in fact impellers which illustrated that he was an ADO (Assistant Divisional Officer) of the Fire Service. This was the equivalent to a Police Chief Inspector. The 'Boss' introduced himself to Art and myself and then proceeded to lead me down the long hill after which we proceeded along the banks of Loch Earn. As I pushed along, I passed the very spot where Chris and I posed for a Lomax photo-shoot more than a year before during an icy winter. I never dreamed at the time that I would one day pass the same venue pushing my chair the length of the country. I had a sudden, deep feeling of nostalgia as I passed and suddenly missed Chris's presence.

As if to compensate my emotions, my mobile phone rang. I suddenly heard the dulcet tones of Chris through my earpiece as she rang to enquire as to my welfare and see how things were progressing. The call lifted my spirits and I told her where it was I had just passed. By now we were passing houses and the ADO decided on a new ploy to generate awareness as to my push to the local population via his vehicle's PA system (public address system). His amplified rhetoric drew people from their homes and gardens. Most, realising I was the one they had seen on the television, then gave very generously. I unequivocally emphasise that the joke depicting the

Scots as being mean is an absolute fallacy. I wish to confirm without any hesitation that the people of Scotland are without doubt very benevolent, hospitable and extremely generous. Finally Art and the 'Boss' escorted me into Comrie where we were greeted by the press and photographers. After another interview and photo-shoot, Art and I were again afforded wonderful hospitality by the fire brigade.

After Art and I washed and changed we were pleasantly surprised when Careen, the wife of Lomax's Executive Director, arrived with her children Catrina and Christie. The reason for the benevolent Careen's visit was so that she could take Art and I to a nearby hotel where she would treat us to a hearty dinner. This unexpected gesture was very much appreciated and all of us thoroughly enjoyed a fantastic meal and wonderful evening making a perfect end to a tiring day. Although I enjoyed my evening and I must admit that the food was excellent, the hotel and its proprietor were the nearest thing to Basil Faulty and his Faulty Towers that I have ever experienced. I hastily add that I found this to be amusing and entertaining. The proprietor first of all told me off for expecting a varied list of soups, 'We've got cream of tomato and that's it!' he snapped. He added, 'I'll give you extra chips and that will fill you'! He tut tutted and cursed every time he passed and tried to negotiate the narrow space I had created by being in a wheelchair and invading his premises. Instead of being offended, I was highly amused, as were the rest of my party as we listened to him snapping at other diners to, 'hurry up' so that he could serve them the next course. We watched as he virtually snatched away dishes from diners who had not quite finished consuming the contents of their plates. He was undoubtedly a worthy contender to follow in the footsteps of John Cleese.

I wish we could have recorded our memorable and highly amusing evening on a video camera. After the meal Art and I thanked Careen and bade her and the children a hearty farewell. Eventually after being so 'lavishly' fed and watered, I retired to the comforts of a nice warm bed. Tomorrow we would be setting off to far away Stirling, and no doubt more exciting adventures!

Chapter Nine
A 'Nocturnal' Fundraising Adventure

Day Twelve

AT 7.30 A.M. I was up and ready for the day's forthcoming trek. Art
and I joined the lads for breakfast, then we set off on the long haul to
distant Stirling. Art wasn't saying much this morning, perhaps his
hormones hadn't fallen into line yet! Art tended to blow 'hot and
cold' on occasions and I soon learned to leave him to it until he would
eventually 'come round'! I felt as though we were really starting to
put some miles behind us now. The weather was kind and the day's
start was a pleasant push through more beautiful countryside. I
pushed alongside a firing range, which reminded me of my period
spent on the Brecon Beacons many years ago. However, all was quiet
and peaceful today. It was a lonely push as I meandered along through
the narrow roads and lanes. Eventually a vehicle belonging to the
National Blood Transfusion Service carefully negotiated the narrow
confines of the carriageway as he passed me. The driver stopped and
alighted from the car and kindly handed me £25. After the usual
friendly chitchat, the gentleman congratulated me on my fundraising
endeavour and wished me every success. He then returned to his
vehicle and drove off and vanished out of sight. As I pushed along I
couldn't help but think it was due entirely to kind and caring people
like him that made my physically demanding efforts so worthwhile.

Eventually, the sparse countryside gave way to wider roads and
houses. I passed a sign which read, 'Auchterarder 4 miles', and again
I felt the pangs of acute nostalgia. The beautiful village of
Auchterarder is the home to the Police Convalescent Home where

Chris and I had been so adequately looked after as I was nursed back to fitness some time ago.

I passed the impressive Wallace Monument, which stood proud among its surrounding trees and foliage. I looked at the great sandstone structure and wondered as to how the hell I had managed to take my wheelchair to the top of such an awe inspiring pinnacle in the past, completing yet another hair raising, fundraising endeavour. My chest swelled with pride to think my successful 'climb' had raised so much money, not to mention a certificate from the Scottish Tourist Authorities. As I pushed further into the outer confines of Stirling, I saw the prone figure of a man lying on a grass verge. I stopped to check if the man was okay. He sat up with difficulty, his eyes were glazed and his speech was slurred. Although the man was clearly under the influence of alcohol, this did not prevent him from instructing me, 'Hey you, C'mere!' The man rose unsteadily to his feet and after grabbing a tree and hanging on to it for support with one hand, he rummaged through his pockets with the other and again commanded, 'Take thish Big Man, Hic! I've seen you on the tele pushin' for cansher'! He handed me a crumpled £20 note. I was loathe to accept this at first due to his condition but not to have done so would undoubtedly have grossly offended him. Drunk or not, he was nevertheless a man of generosity. I accepted his donation and as I made my way on toward the town the drunk plonked himself down again on the grass and shouted, 'Good on yer Big Man'.

Art, having been in contact with Stirling Fire Station, must have arranged for an escort into town. Suddenly, two fire engines sounded their klaxons as they came out of a side road to join us. One took up a position ahead of me, the other astern, Art remaining at the rear. The crews of each machine 'baled out' to join me. Our procession wandered into and through the bustling and busy historic Scottish town. Our trek had obviously received constant publicity prior to our arrival, which then in turn generated the interest of those witnessing our arrival. Money poured into the buckets being carried by the optimistically prepared Stirling fire crews.

Lady donor outside Stirling Fire Station

Finally, after the rapid and steep descent down below the walls of the impressive Stirling Castle fortress, which now loomed high above us, we arrived at Stirling Fire Station. There, press and TV cameras greeted us. A tearful young lady carrying a baby stopped me. Her husband accompanied her. Both hugged me and the lady explained that the couple had experienced the inconsolable loss of their young daughter to cancer and insisted that I took the two £20 notes she offered. As I accepted the money cameras popped and the TV filmed the emotional gesture. Again, this illustrated the importance of such a fundraising motive. I felt *very* humble indeed, yet extremely proud of what I was doing in my Marje's treasured memory. I was more determined than ever that this long distance 'first' would be a successful and financial accomplishment. Many other people also gathered and donated copious amounts of money to swell the fund. Eventually Art and I were ushered inside the station and given a much-appreciated hot mug of tea. Press interviews were finally concluded and the station returned to normal.

Art and I made our way to the canteen where we befriended the station's mascot, a chocolate brown Labrador dog call Sam.

As we sat enjoying our mug of tea, we were pleasantly surprised when in walked George Murray, the Superintendent in charge at Auchterarder Police Convalescent Home, with his wife Gill. Both joined us at the table and each were immediately furnished with a cup of tea by our station hosts. Their visit was very much appreciated and was certainly a real morale booster to me, especially at the end of such a long and tiring day. After George and Gill left us, Art and I were taken to the Grangemouth Dockers' Club to attend a social evening. Unknown to Art and I, this had been arranged by the Stirling Fire Brigade. All present made both Art and I extremely welcome and Art was 'forced' to drink copious amounts of beer by the evening's revellers! I was handed a substantial sum of money that had been donated by the club and its members, after which I addressed all present from the stage and thanked them profusely. Also present was a young lady, Mandy Robertson, who I was privileged to meet.

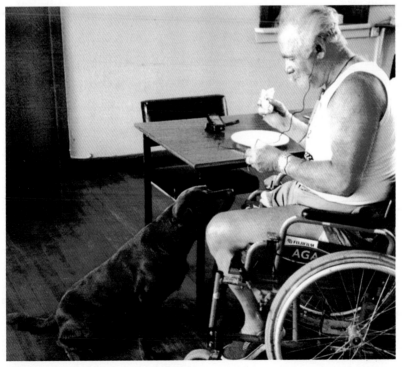

Swasie and Stirling F.S. mascot 'Sam'

Mandy was shortly to climb the famous Mount Kilimanjaro for charity. She too was handed a large donation for her cause.

After spending an extremely pleasant hour among the benevolent Dockers and their families, we returned to Stirling Fire Station. There, we washed and changed then tucked into a hearty meal with the lads. The enterprising firefighter on kitchen duty, the day's cook, brought the lads' dinners of sausage, chips and beans in and placed them on the table before them. He then brought my 'dinner' in. At this stage I must inform everyone who is not aware and privy to life in the services, we in the services are traditionally blessed with a (sick) sense of humour and tonight would be no exception. He placed a large glass container containing my *liquefied* dinner on the table before me, then removed my knife and fork, 'in case I harmed myself'! My sausage and chips had been put through a *blender* first! The firefighter audaciously justified this by informing me, 'With you being in a wheelchair, I thought it would be better for you this way'! Everyone present, and I emphasise that this *included* myself, fell about with laughter on seeing my meal in a glass with a large straw sticking out of the top. Gesticulating to him with my two fingers I immediately advised him to call at the 'Foreign Office' forthwith! This 'canteen culture' and service banter thankfully prevails and many times is a *very* effective safety valve after attending traumatic incidents.

Later, on a more serious note, whilst we were dining, a couple of kind, enterprising firefighters, thinking of my comforts, brought down a bed to save me negotiating the stairs later. What a kind thought and what a great bunch of people. This is absolutely *typical* of our brilliant services. That is why I remain *fiercely* loyal to all our truly *great* British emergency services. Without doubt, they are the world's *greatest!*

Not content with the weight of the cash contained in the buckets after the day's takings were checked, the station's boss, a young enterprising Station Officer, suggested a visit into town to visit Stirling's pubs. I reluctantly pointed out the fact that I was a non-drinker but I obviously didn't get his drift and appreciate what he had in mind. The officer quickly enlightened me, saying, 'No, I don't mean to go on the ale Swasie, I mean to go collecting from all the pubs'! To this I heartily and gratefully agreed. The officer had some guts as he did no more than turn out a couple of machines and I accompanied a junior officer in the station's ET (emergency tender). Stirling was busy that night. Throngs of drinkers drifted from pub to pub, (as we did with our buckets!). In most pubs, the females seemed to be hell bent on separating the firefighters from their uniforms! 'Strategic parts' of the lads' anatomy were unceremoniously grabbed, groped and fondled by the ladies, whilst others tore at the firefighters' clothing. Chants of 'OFF! OFF! OFF!' rang through the various establishments we visited. These chants were however, generously accompanied by substantial cash donations which flowed into the buckets. I witnessed a young woman grab the Leading Firefighter and insist that he inspect her tattoos as she exposed her (very ample) bare breasts. Each breast bore a tattoo near its nipple. On seeing their friend do this, other women did likewise and exposed their ample charms also, each of the women vying for a position near to a firefighter. Sitting in a wheelchair, I appeared to be either very vulnerable – or – at an acute advantage should any collisions occur! However, being very brave I wasn't frightened! Needless to say, the evening was thoroughly enjoyable and extremely financially successful. What a 'Trip Ashore' and night on the Town that was! What an inspiring initiative by the Station Officer.

At the conclusion of the night's 'Fundraising operations' we all returned to the station for supper. Art again busied himself logging the mileage and reporting on the day's activities then counting the day's donations, which, due to the evening's activities, proved *extremely* substantial.

Finally, bedtime and we all retired for the night. Unfortunately, during the early hours there were a couple of 'shouts' so the lads' night slumbers were not to remain undisturbed. However, what a *perfect* end to a great day!

TIP TO TOE

Day Thirteen

Up and washed by 6.50 a.m., Art brought me a cuppa. After breakfast with the day shift, Art and I started our long trek to Slamannan. Tonight we would be staying at 'state of the art' Falkirk Fire Station. We were escorted again through Stirling and yet again the money flowed from the donations by tireless and selfless people who appreciated what we were doing and why. Eventually our escort left us approximately five miles outside Stirling. We still had 20 miles to go yet, and there were a lot of *extremely* steep hills to negotiate at journey's end at the conclusion of today's push!

After many miles had passed beneath my casters, a lady approached me and asked if I would follow her down a side street in the little village of Eirth. I did as I was asked and followed the lady until we reached a school. Lining the pavement outside the school were nearly two hundred children. Their shouts and screams of welcome were heard before I caught sight of the happy throng. The lady turned out to be the mother of Anne Matherson (Glencoe Tea Room) who was then joined by Anne's aunt and the headmistress of the school Jessie and her teacher colleagues. I was subject to a tumultuous welcome, which was not only unexpected but also extremely touching.

As I entered the playground at the request of Jessie, the kids immediately mobbed me. Photographs were taken by the score by Art and teachers alike. I felt like some sort of celebrity pop star, such was the ovation we received by those lovely little children. I felt embarrassed as many of the children asked for my autograph. I was, nevertheless, immensely proud and again humbled, at such a greeting. We received generous donations from teachers, neighbours and dinner ladies and, eventually, after our happy 'pit stop' Art and I (reluctantly) left the happy children and continued our trek on to Slamannan.

After completing over 18 miles, during which I received many donations from motorists and local inhabitants of the places I passed through, I then had to negotiate one of the longest, steepest climbs ever. It was horrendous. The long, steep drag took what seemed an age. So steep was the gradient that I had to stop to allow the strength back into my upper arms and shoulders. I was sweating buckets, which ran down my arms causing my hands to become wet and slippy. This made pushing my wheels more difficult. A lady (who was the widow of a local firefighter and who worked at the station where we would be staying that night) came out of her house with a most welcome glass of chilled water. I 'plundered' the contents of the glass ruthlessly before requesting more. The lady gladly obliged and after a short natter, I continued with the difficult ascent up the steep hill. Finally, at long last, the three-mile long hill was successfully climbed. After what seemed an eternity, we entered the little village of Slamannan and made for the small fire station. As we turned into the station's road, a crowd of villagers and children cheered us home and greeted Art and I with warm affection. We were then ushered inside the station and saw that the ladies of the village had been very busy prior to our arrival.

A table had be more than adequately furnished with cakes, pies, sandwiches, jellies, and a large pot of tea, lemonade, orange juice and other equally mouth-watering fare. The local press also attended and again, many photographs were taken during the press interview. I was presented with a bottle of whisky and £20 for the bucket.

After our wonderful welcome and reception, Art drove us to Falkirk Fire Station where we were to spend the night before resuming from Slamannon in the morning. The ADO's wife kindly took my clothes to wash and would return them all, crisp and clean the following morning. That evening the Sub Officer of the night watch cooked the tea but unfortunately, just as we started to eat, the bells went down and the lads had to make a hasty exit from the station leaving Art and I to eat alone while they attended a 'shout'. At least I was given an ordinary plate and real knife and fork this time! Having worked in the fire service it came as second nature for me to gather all their meals and return them to the oven to await their return.

Later that night, Chris rang and I then tended to my split hands. I awaited the return of the lads before finally retiring to my bed. I was so tired I went out like a light as soon as my head touched the pillow.

Day Fourteen

After a great night's sleep I was up again like the proverbial lark at 7.30 a.m. My hands felt okay after yesterday's battering and I was again raring to go! We were slowly but surely now getting down towards the elusive England. After breakfast with the 'troops', the lads (and the ADO) escorted me while we wandered through Falkirk's pedestrian precinct. The sight of 'our gang', me with flags flying from my chair, the lads, and the ADO carrying buckets, certainly generated a lot of interest. The shoppers donated generously with cash, and many ladies kindly gave much appreciated hugs and kisses, even some for me! We then set off on our day's 24 mile push to Carluke. First I had to fulfil a promise I made to the children of Slamannan yesterday, that I would call in to their school

Soaking wet Swasie talks to Slamanan schoolchildren

to give them a little talk regarding my 'chair-borne adventures'. I was now being escorted by a fire engine as I pushed along, and as I neared the little primary school the heavens suddenly opened with a vengeance. Torrential rain cascaded down relentlessly. Soon a torrential river flowed down the steep main street forming waterfalls as it relentlessly wept across the pavements and steps. My escort suggested that it would be better if I carried on due to my thorough soaking. However, I wouldn't hear of it. There was no way I could let the little mites down. I entered the school and pushed into the assembly hall. It's as well I did because all the children were sitting cross-legged awaiting my arrival. As I sat and faced them a pool of water completely surrounded me as I dripped, what seemed, gallons onto the highly polished floor.

After my talk I asked if there were any questions. One typically inquisitive youngster put his hand up and asked, 'How did yer lose yer leg?' I told him I had been 'run over'. The indignant little boy then chastised me and said, 'Well it serves you right, it wouldn't have happened if you'd stopped and looked both ways and listened like you're supposed to'! His embarrassed teachers tried (in vain) to stifle their laughter at his rebuke. I was highly amused by his naïve audacity and I could see Art and the firefighters were also.

We left the little gathering and resumed our journey towards distant England. It was still raining heavily and water was cascading down the gutters as I made my way up and down the steep hills. Eventually the rain stopped and things got a little better, although the blustery winds were a bit of a pain. I received a number of calls on my mobile from friends and the media. These calls helped to consume time and boost morale.

One call was from an ex-prison officer pal, Robbie Collister. Robbie was assisting me with a book I was writing entitled *A Cop on Rule 43*, his assistance being very much appreciated, as was his call now. We lost our escort after five miles and Art was now my sole protector. As I passed along a quiet country road I heard the sound of an animal in distress. Eventually I found the source of the cries.

Looking under a hedge I saw that a young lamb had got its head well and truly tangled amongst brambles and wire fencing and was stuck fast. I pushed myself over and even as I tried in vain to free the poor little thing his bleating was already getting weaker. Art, driving behind and seeing me suddenly veer off course across the road must have wondered what on earth I was doing diving into a bunch of nettles at the base of a prickly hedge. He joined me and together our joint efforts eventually managed to free the frightened and bleeding lamb. We had to cut a tight wire 'noose' and some twigs away from its neck to get the animal free. Art then mended the fence and we resumed our trek. Had we not come across the lamb at that crucial time, there is no doubt it would have choked to death within a very short time. Thankfully, I was in the right place at the right time.

Our day's lengthy and eventful push was eventually successfully completed and we arrived at our overnight refuge at Carluke at 5.30 p.m. The station's Sub Officer who was about to go off duty warmly greeted us. After the shift change the night parade (Red Watch) came on duty.

Our meal tonight was sweet and sour chicken. The fire service certainly contains many who are more than capable of creating a 'chef-d'oeuvre' when required to do so! I received calls from Chris and my daughter Jo then settled down to watch a bit of television. Art and I were again treated to fantastic hospitality. The Brigade was yet again spoiling us when they placed two beds downstairs especially for us. Eventually the day drew to a close and we all made for our beds. Our presence on the stations must have been a jinx as there were always 'shouts' during the night when things were *usually* quiet! Tonight was again to be no exception as the crews' slumbers were to be disturbed on two occasions.

Day Fifteen

At 7.25 a.m. I awoke to the sound of the crews' morning ablutions and looking out of the window I saw that the day looked bright and

Donors from coach on Highland Road

promising. Art was still snoring like an enraged bull. Finally Art rose and we made our way in for breakfast. We were now the guests of Blue Watch (my old watch). After a full English breakfast the Brigade and press held a photo shoot outside the station on the road. Pictures were taken alongside the machines, the crews and senior officers.

Today's haul was to be a long one. The push was to Elvanfoot, a distance of just under 30 miles. The bonus today however, was that the weather was fine and looked as if it would last. Motherwell would today furnish our escort in the form of a Brigade Land Rover. Although the vehicle was fitted with a PA system, this was not utilised. Nevertheless, prior media publicity would hopefully cater for filling our coffers during the day's push.

I received many donations from motorists, local people and residents as I passed them by. Staff and customers alike emerged from shops and garden centres to hand their donations to me. I passed through Coatbridge and on to struggle up the long climb to, and through, Lanark. The two-mile climb up and through Lanark was very stamina-sapping as the climb seemed never ending and was very steep.

After passing through the town and finally reaching the top and 'levelling out', I stopped to accept donations from a couple of youths who were in their school uniform. They were eating chips during their school lunch break and I asked them to go for a bag of chips for me. I sat at the roadside talking to them and eating my chips before carrying on. Except for the two boys' donations, I received nothing from the people of Lanark. Perhaps things would have been different had the Land Rover's PA system been used as we passed through the town. I have a friendly neighbour, Wilma Palmer, who originates from Lanark and I (jokingly) now refer to her hometown as 'Tightlanark'!

I had an insatiable thirst as I pushed but persevered and pushed on until I made my destination and made for the retained fire station at Douglas. The station's crew, although retained, nevertheless, left their homes or various places of employment to be there to greet us on our arrival. We were taken to a local 'chippy' and treated to a large meal of fish and chips. I think I must have drunk the town dry to satisfy my thirst. Later Divisional Officer Charlie Welsh and Assistant Divisional Officer Craige Shaw arrived at the station to meet us. They, together with Firefighter Alan 'Smokey' Aitkin presented me with a souvenir Ben Fund moneybox and a Brigade shield. During our little 'ceremony' my new Lomax driver, Grant, arrived together with the Lomax factory foreman Bob, as tomorrow Art would be leaving me for two weeks training with the Territorial Army down in Worcestershire. Art is a 'Rasman', (a Regimental Sergeant Major). At the conclusion of the evening's activities the officers left, and the station once more became quiet and deserted except for myself and my Lomax pals. The station was warm and comfortable and eventually the four of us managed to settle down (on the floor) and get some sleep. This peace and tranquillity was not to last for long however! Yet again, we were to become the station jinx! During the night both machines were turned out to a fire.

Chapter Ten
Onward with my New Lomax Escort 'Pilot'

Day Sixteen

I WAS FULLY awake at 6.45 a.m. after an uncomfortable and restless night's sleep. I slid my aching frame out of my sleeping bag and lifted myself into my 'second home', my chair! I must admit to being a little apprehensive at the thought of losing Art today. Although he was sometimes cantankerous and moaned a lot, I knew I would miss him all the same. He had looked after me well during the last 15 days of my grunting, soaking, sweating pushes, which so far had covered over 280 miles and raised over £2,000. I sincerely hoped young Grant could offer and administer the same 'tender, loving care' to his wheelchair-bound charge.

Art was up early and after furnishing us all with a hot brew, he proceeded to brief Grant as to the do's and don'ts, the routes and stopovers, as well as acquainting him with various other bits and bobs to ensure that all would run smoothly during the two weeks of his absence. Grant listened intently, absorbing all as well as familiarising himself with the paperwork Art had started. Art kindly decided that he and Bob would travel in convoy and accompany us as far as the end of the day's push. I think Grant appreciated this as it would 'break him in' as to our routine and procedure. A number of the local people, many of them children, had gathered outside the fire station to bid us farewell. After another hot, sweet brew of tea had been consumed the friendly group saw us off after handing us yet more kind donations. A number of photographs of us and the gathering were taken to record our departure, then our little convoy, led by the flag-

Looking down on Swasie on long road

decked wheelchair, set off into the warm, sunny and pleasant
morning. Today we were making for Lockerbie, 27 miles away.

Even after pushing for most of the day, Lockerbie never seemed
to get any nearer. After I had pushed non-stop for nearly 20 miles, I
was making my way along a very quiet and long, almost endless, dead
straight stretch of road when suddenly a car passed me before
stopping further along the road. As I neared the vehicle, out stepped

a firefighter and his wife from Slamannan. They had driven out specially to intercept me so that they could present me with another £120 they had collected from their colleagues on the station back home after we left them. What fantastic people I was having the privilege of rubbing shoulders with!

After more long, steep hills (and a couple of downpours) we finally arrived at the beautiful village of Lockerbie. It was here that, with a wave and a salute, Art finally took his leave of us. Grant and I sadly waved him off on his own long journey South to 'Soldierland'. As I had now concluded the day's mileage, Grant and I made our way to our 'home for the night' at Dumfries Fire Station.

After a wash and brush up and a change into dry clothing, Grant and I were unexpectedly visited by Chris; a Lomax employee who is sadly now no longer with us. As Chris was in the vicinity he decided to call and take Grant and I out for a meal.

He kindly took us to a nearby Berni's Inn where he treated us both to a wonderful steak dinner. While I was under the anaesthetic of gastronomic enchantment, I received a phone call from Mrs Matherson and Sir Jimmy Saville at Glencoe wishing me well on my long fundraising journey. What a nice gesture by the two to have been so thoughtful. Later, after the evening's socialising drew to a close, Grant and I returned to our fire station. After thanking our generous and considerate host Chris, truly an 'Officer and a Gentleman' *and* a Jewel in the Lomax crown who is well and truly missed, Grant and I crept into the station to make to our beds. However, there was no need for our silent endeavours as the lads were up playing snooker and watching television. We were spotted and invited to join them for a cup of tea. Grant and I joined them before we all eventually retired. I was still a little apprehensive and worried if Grant would be as efficient as Art.

The next two weeks would illustrate how my fears would be well and truly unfounded. Finally, after our nightcap, Grant and I made for our beds and, once I was beneath the sheets I was instantly asleep.

Chapter Eleven
Leaving St. Andrew to Join St. George

Day Seventeen

SUNDAY, 4TH JUNE. The whole watch were excited for me and warmly congratulated me knowing that today I was at last pushing into *England*! I found it difficult to accept that at the end of today I would have propelled myself, unaided, through the whole length of bonnie Scotland in an ordinary castered wheelchair. I had now literally successfully pushed sixteen, consecutive, non-stop London Marathons. After a hearty breakfast, courtesy of the Dumfries Fire Service, I set off again from Lockerbie with Grant close behind. I had to tell Grant to fall further behind to ensure that motorists were given adequate warning of my presence further ahead of him. Although the weather was dull and grey together with the occasional drop of rain that fell, the elements didn't diminish or lower my high morale on this landmark and most memorable of days.

Grant very soon got into the swing of things and started to show his true colours. He quickly illustrated what a concerned, efficient and caring back-up he was. When he thought I should have a drink he would ring me or draw alongside and furnish me with the appropriate 'nectar'. The day later started to warm up considerably. Grant suddenly passed me and vanished over the horizon. A short time later he reappeared with a most welcome ice-lolly. I could tell we were going to get on well! I was making good progress as the day wore on and as I passed through the outskirts of Kirkpatrick I met a couple of cyclists who were 'going the other way' on *their* 'end-to-end'. We stopped for a brief chat and exchanged pleasantries before I

Swasie enters Gretna Green

resumed my slog South. My adrenaline flowed, as I knew we were nearing Gretna Green, and subsequently – England!

As I travelled along a quiet and empty road a police car approached me from the opposite direction. The vehicle passed me but I saw its brake lights flash in my mirror. The car turned round and drew alongside me. The driver (Andy) introduced himself and his observer (Colin) to me. Andy told me that he had been following my progress via the media and also that he recognised me from my column in the *Police News*. As always, I was overjoyed to be rubbing shoulders with my colleagues (the 'Cloth') and I asked Grant to hand them a copy of my book *Wheelchair Pilot* which he carried in the van. The police crew then joined us and escorted me the last couple of miles into Gretna.

On arrival, we stopped and had a welcome cuppa amongst the tourists, many of whom were fascinated on seeing a vest and shorts-clad 'end-to-ender' in a wheelchair with flags flying, passing through the little village. At this time I received a call from Radio Forth on my mobile. I was then interviewed live on air and related my many adventures whilst travelling through Scotland and its Highlands. Many of the people who gathered round me were aware of my trek and gave generously. Some of the tourists were from my neck of the woods on the Wirral and Merseyside. Our police escort then wished us well before leaving us to resume their patrol, but not before they too, gave a generous donation to our coffers. Grant and I had a quick wander around the souvenir shop and it was then that a fire tender and crew joined us.

The Sub Officer in charge of the machine suggested that he escort us down to a nearby shopping mall. He thought we would collect a lot of money there if we all wandered amongst the shoppers. This was a great idea and I pushed down the steep hill escorted by some of the fire crew who walked alongside me. We reached the shopping mall and as the driver parked his machine a uniformed security officer approached us. The Sub Officer informed the man of our fundraising intentions and as a matter of courtesy sought his permission to do so. The security officer, obviously unable to make such a 'life or death' decision, timidly requested us to 'stand by' while he contacted his boss on the radio. His boss, having been given such an *astronomical* decision to make, could clearly be heard huffing and puffing before instructing his subordinate, ' – er, okay, er, very well, but tell them to put the fire engine down at the bottom of the car park out of the way'. The indignant Sub Officer took the hapless security officer's radio and proceeded to insert loud decibels of forthright rhetoric into the instrument, informing the self important and pompous 'Jobs Worth' – 'The bloody fire engine is staying where it is!', elaborating in no uncertain terms the importance of it being accessible should the need arise. The Sub concluded his radio rendition with the finale, *'Bloody Tosspot!'*, which was undoubtedly a correct description. The timid and by now appeasing security officer readily agreed with the firefighter and uttered, 'Good on yer mate' as he retrieved his red hot radio from the irate Sub Officer.

Our wander around the stores generated very little in the way of cash so we decided to move on. After thanking our optimistic and enterprising fire crew for their efforts and company, Grant and I bade them farewell as we made for the nearby 'Border'.

As I reached another well-known tourist attraction on the Border, namely the 'Last House in Scotland', a motorist stopped me. The driver got out of his car and asked if he and his family could be photographed with me alongside the famous house. I was more than happy to oblige and Grant took pictures for our own record as well as those for the motorist.

Before leaving us the gentleman and his family thanked Grant and I and congratulated us both for what we were doing. He then handed Grant £20 for our bucket before making off into England. As I moved off, a female ex-police colleague (who I assisted with her first arrest many years ago in Liverpool) also pleasantly surprised me by pulling in to talk to me. What a wonderful surprise to see her again after so many years and especially at such a venue during my marathon push.

Finally, after a long push, I rolled down the main street of Longtown before finally rolling across the concrete apron in front of Longtown Fire Station. There, waiting to greet me was a Leading Firefighter. I was greeted with a firm, warm handshake, 'Hi, my name's Bill Kirkup' said my new host. Bill's arms were like young oaks. He was built like a brick privy! His warm, kind and friendly

Entering England

welcome illustrated that his formidable size belied the fact that he was actually a 'gentle giant'. Bill took Grant and I into his spacious bungalow next door to the fire station. There, Grant and I were introduced to his charming wife Ruth who afforded us an equally warm and friendly welcome.

Very soon the charming couple's young son Joe, clad in his own firefighter's outfit joined us with his younger brother. It was obvious what seven-year-old Joe's ultimate ambitions were! In no time we were sat at the table and furnished with a scrumptious dinner that would have filled a horse. We were also joined at the table by Bill's boss, the Station Officer who is also a family friend. Ruth fussed about and ensured that Grant and I would need a crane to remove us from the table.

Although it had been arranged that Grant and I would sleep in the fire station before returning to the bungalow for breakfast the following morning, Ruth decided that we should sleep in the bungalow and sorted two beds out (from nowhere) to facilitate this. I was by now feeling the strain of the day's activities and decided to 'crash out' for the night at 9.30 p.m. Not so for Grant! He went out with Big Bill and the lads for a few pints. I had now pushed nearly 370 miles and the money raised had topped over £3,800.

Swasie and young 'FM Kirkup', Longtown

Chapter Twelve
Oh to be Back Home in England

Day Eighteen

AFTER A GREAT night's sleep Grant and I were woken by the lovely Ruth who handed us a cup of tea to start the day. It looked as though Grant too had inherited my 'jinx' as the lads were called out to a fire during the night; the only 'nocturnal' shout this week! The night's activity had escaped me, as I didn't hear a thing!

After a hearty breakfast of bacon, eggs, beans, toast, bread and butter and the proverbial copious amounts of tea (Oh boy! They *certainly do* know how to eat in Longtown!) Grant and I sadly said goodbye to the our wonderful hosts of Longtown (who remain my very close friends to this day).

Having been filled to bursting with our early morning's gastronomic delights, I popped next door into the Station Watch Room to endorse the station memo book prior to our departure. Grant then followed me as I pushed back along Longtown High Street before turning right and heading on and out of town. Generous early morning shoppers and townsfolk kindly continued to fill my bucket as I passed them by. I was now pushing on South to my next 'Port of Call' at Carlisle, many miles (and many hours) away. Today's push seemed to be one long, continual climb. There didn't seem to be any respite in my grunting, sweating and aching, ongoing uphill pushes. When I *did* have the comfort of a level or downhill push, this was again, followed by yet another seemingly never-ending uphill stretch. It was just as well that Ruth insisted on me having a big breakfast to sustain strength and stamina during my strenuous endeavours.

Eventually I was pushing along an extremely busy, wide and fast highway; almost a motorway. The heavy lorries thundered by and now it was raining, it added to the delirious fun I was having by being saturated by the icy cold spray as they passed. I was now becoming highly amused! As my wet and slow slog progressed further, I started to get the feeling that perhaps I was beginning to suffer an acute sense of humour loss – again!

I pressed on, thoroughly enjoying life in general as the rain just wouldn't let up! Although I was sweating, I was also cold due to being soaked through to the skin. Eventually, the town of Penrith came into view. A couple of miles and three quarters of an hour later I passed the sign welcoming me to the town, I'm sure *that* must have bucked me up no end!

As I pushed on into the town proper there were some who, on seeing the drenched wheelchair pilot, gave generously to my bucket. I must admit, their kind generosity and a bit of banter did help to lift my spirits. I continued on through the busy town's labyrinth of narrow and extremely congested streets, to which I no doubt contributed considerably. My slow, crawling presence was undoubtedly causing sheer delight to bus drivers, taxi drivers and motorists as I plodded on through the town.

Lady donor on outskirts of Penrith in the rain

As I laboriously pushed on up another little 'steepie' I received an endearing call from Chris on my mobile. Although her calls were always appreciated morale boosters, it was very awkward and stamina-sapping when trying to talk and hold a conversation whilst pushing up a steep hill.

After hours of non-stop pushing I was enjoying a long downhill roll when a man stepped out into the road in front of me. I stopped and the man handed me a £10 note and, pointing to the nearby 'Terracotta Restaurant' he informed me that he was its owner and invited Grant and I in for a meal. Although I was not ready for a meal, I told him I would appreciate a long, cold drink. The extremely kind gentleman, Mr Stephen Hoolickin, ushered Grant and I inside his very lavish establishment and furnished us both with drinks of iced lemonade, which was nothing less than pure nectar! Our host then presented me with a bottle of champagne before insisting that he generously stocked our van with cold drinks, sweets and chocolate, as well as an abundant supply of savouries. Our unexpected benefactor was more than pleased when all I could do in return was present him with a signed copy of *Wheelchair Pilot*.

After half an hour, thoroughly refreshed, we thanked Mr Hoolickin profusely for his *more than generous* hospitality, then resumed our trek. As we reached the outskirts of the town, due to Grant's constant updates to our host stations, a Carlisle fire engine escort met us. They kindly guided us into town through the one way system until we reached the main pedestrian shopping precinct. There we stopped and the crew dismounted from their machine. We all ventured through the crowds of shoppers with our buckets. As always, our fire service is well liked and appreciated by the public and again, this was emphasised by the many generous donations we received as we wandered amongst them. After our buckets were substantially 'weighted' we all made to Brampton Fire Station – our 'digs' for the night.

On arrival Sub Officer Vince Jobson met us and kindly 'settled us in'. After a wash and change Grant and I were informed that one of the retained firefighters from our station, Mr Phil Hellington, was the manager of the nearby Howard Arms Hotel. Mr Hellington insisted on looking after us for the evening by inviting us both to his hotel for dinner.

Whilst we were enjoying our substantial meal, a 'Road Gang' was drinking in the bar. They became aware of our presence and the reason for our being in town and we were cordially invited to join them at the conclusion of our meal. On joining them, I was delighted to find that a number of them were Welsh. This gave me an excuse to talk to them in their own 'language of the valleys' having learned to speak Welsh at night school.

Grant and I got on well with the gang and they insisted we attend there the following morning for breakfast before we set off on our day's push. Finally the evening ended and, after filling numerous containers with cash donations, our hosts and new friends bid us 'Nos Da' (goodnight). A rather inebriated Grant and a teetotal Swasie returned to the station and 'hit the sack'.

Day Nineteen

After a good night's sleep, as promised, Grant the Scot and Swasie of St George joined the 'united nations' gang at the hotel for breakfast. After topping up with gastronomic fuel we left our friends to much ribald banter (as well as receiving yet more donations) and returned to the fire station. I endorsed the Watch Room memo book then Grant and I set off again.

Our journey today would take us as far as the little village of Shap where we would call a halt before resuming on to Kendal the next day. As soon as I started my push the heavens opened and I was soon a very wet and brassed off unhappy wanderer! The steep hills started almost right away to add to my acute discomfort. My push took me along a very busy major road and yet again I *enjoyed* the incessant freezing cold showers of dirty spray as the steady stream of speeding lorries continued unabated. It was at times like this that I wondered if

Swasie climbs up Shap

I was 'in possession of my marbles'! I knew I must maintain my self-discipline as there were still many, *many* hundreds of miles to go. I snapped myself out of my bad-tempered lethargy and continued on. A motorist stopped and came to me in the pouring rain. I was delighted to once again meet an old police colleague from the past. We had served together in Liverpool many years before and my friend had since retired and become a licensee.

His pub was just a few miles further along the road and I was cordially invited to call in for a beer. I politely declined his offer as time was of the essence and I was cold and wet, plus the fact that I was a 'non-drinker'. I was invited to call in just the same, as my friend would ensure that there would be a number of donations forthcoming from his customers.

He led by example and kindly handed me a £20 note before driving off into the spray to warn his customers of my pending arrival. Needless to say, I did call at my friend's neat little roadside tavern where I was inundated with copious amounts of cash from his generous patrons. Ever onward, I continued pushing ever upwards as the many, energy sapping climbs passed beneath my wheels (and casters). Finally, I entered the Lake District's picturesque little village of Shap, hidden in one of Cumbria's most isolated areas. The beautiful village, with its grazing sheep and granite quarry also has a medieval abbey. Another three miles would take me through the village and on to the top of the infamous 'Shap Fell' where I would, thankfully, conclude the day's push.

As I entered the village the rain stopped and the clouds began to clear, allowing the sun to shine through. The heat from the sun was gratefully received and I started to warm up a bit. I saw a pub on the opposite side of the road. Some drinkers came outside and gathered in the sunshine as I approached. I saw that one of them was in a wheelchair. On seeing wheelchairs, it is always my policy to greet the occupants, whatever their state of communicative comprehension. I crossed over and went to the group. All were very sociable and asked about my presence in their village. I explained and immediately they all offered donations from coins to notes, each gratefully received. I offered my hand to the young man in a wheelchair but he knocked it away then turned and propelled his wheelchair back inside the pub. 'Take no notice', said one of the group. He went on to explain that the young man, once a keen motorcyclist, had been knocked off his machine and as a result had lost his left foot. Due to this he was very bitter and sadly blamed the 'world and his dog' for his predicament. I thanked the gang for their kind donations then resumed my push to the summit of Shap.

On arrival at the 1,400 ft summit I stopped to admire the wonderful panoramic view laid out before me. I was more than ready to return to Penrith Fire Station for our evening meal and night's sleep before carrying on from here tomorrow. Boy! Was I ready to eat and sleep! As Grant drove us back along what had been my day's cold and wet route, I rang my daughter Jo to inform her of how my push was progressing.

On arrival at the fire station I enjoyed the sheer luxury of a hot bath after the day's nine hour, 20-mile push. After changing into

Outside Jubilee House

warm, dry clothing, Grant and I were invited for dinner by the staff at Jubilee House, the luxurious and extremely therapeutic Fire Services' Convalescent Home. The home is situated in beautiful surroundings on the banks of a Salmon River on the outskirts of Penrith. We were highly honoured and immensely proud to be dining with the home's heroic patients of 'broken firefighters'.

The cuisine would do a four star hotel proud. At the conclusion of our meal the home's Matron gave Grant and I a conducted tour of the very impressive establishment. Many memorable photographs were taken including some alongside the fast flowing river and its thundering waterfall. During my visit I sold copies of my books, *Off the Cuff* (my autobiography) and *Wheelchair Pilot*, the profits from these books again going into the bucket!

I had earlier been contacted by the Television News requesting a televised interview and pictures of me pushing my chair along the road. I readily agreed and specifically asked that they attend at Jubilee House in order to give the establishment, and its heroes, well deserved television coverage. I wanted the world to see that firefighters do get seriously injured performing their heroic duties. They promised me they would attend. Sadly, as I have found to be typical of the press and media, unless anything is for their own benefit, rarely do they fulfil their promises! Needless to say, the T. V. news crew did *not* appear!

Eventually we reluctantly left the home and its heroes and returned to our station. I left Grant watching television with the lads and made for my bed. It was not long before I was fast asleep inside the warm duvet. I needed my rest, as it would be hard going tomorrow!

Chapter Thirteen
Continual Warm Hospitality, but more Inexcusable Bad Manners

Day Twenty

UNKNOWN TO ME, there were two other overnight guests on the station. There were two firefighters from the Cumbrian Brigade, Alan Lamb and Mike Robinson who were in the process of cycling the 'Coast to Coast' run (West to East across England) for charity. It was one of them, Mike, who handed me a hot mug of tea and a sausage sandwich, after waking me from my slumbers.

Today the weather looked promising. As we left our host station the sky was devoid of cloud and threats of yesterday's inclement behaviour. First, I relished in the comforts of the warm van as Grant drove to the top of 'Shap Fell' where I would resume my push.

On our subsequent arrival at the (not too warm) summit I settled into my chariot once again. I surveyed the very steep and long, winding descent that I would be negotiating. Looking further into the distance I saw with horror the equally long, winding and steep climb I would have once I had completed my lengthy descent. Even Grant expressed his trepidation at the thought of my forthcoming endurance. 'Bloody hell, sooner you than me Swasie', he said. 'Mind you, it's nothing you can't handle' he added as kind, encouraging consolation. I set off with a gentle push and soon I was having to grip my wheels and tyres tightly as the forces of gravity manifested themselves. Even though the motorway has eliminated the need for most vehicular traffic on Shap, there were still cars and lorries travelling both ways and I needed to be alert and aware of the potential danger from them at all times.

Swasie descends Shap's steep drop

Soon, my hands were beginning to burn as I tried to maintain a slow descent. Once the chair exceeded three miles per hour the little front casters would violently vibrate from side to side. This would then cause the chair to either stop dead or turn violently to the right or left. Should I inadvertently allow any of these manoeuvres to occur, I would undoubtedly be thrown from my chair. I learned this *very* early, soon after I started to 'inhabit' my chariot! After my lengthy descent and a couple of collisions with the unforgiving, sheer rock face at the roadside (due to violent swerves to the left!) most of the palms of my (one and a half) hands were devoid of skin. Many would no doubt consider that the use of gloves would be an appropriate form of attire, however I consider gloves not only to be cumbersome and a hindrance but they also soften the skin, whereas my hands were now normally like leather. Due to my preference therefore, I would have to bear the consequences. Before I started my lengthy climb up the other side I stopped and bound my hands with plastic insulation tape for further protection. This was better than plasters as it was strong, elastic and totally waterproof. Even heavy perspiration did not cause loss of adhesion. Although not the most hygienic of hand-dressing protection, it sufficed! I forced my bursting arms to propel my heavy chair up past a set of roadworks. I moved inside the cones to allow vehicles to get past. Some of the wide-eyed workmen (who were obviously not aware of the efforts I was undertaking) did come across and hand me cash donations on learning what I was up to out there in the wilderness. Motorists also stopped and gave generously. Even out there in the middle of nowhere, my bucket was constantly and very generously being 'fed'!

All seemed to be going well when, once again, along came the rain. Oh good, another soaking! However, my misery was short-lived. In the distance I saw the welcome, heart lifting sight of 'Fireman Sam' in the form of two approaching fire engines. The leading machine flashed its lights then they both stopped before turning round to join us. The officer in charge, Sub Officer Bruce Greenbank informed Grant and I that being aware of our approach to Kendal they had come to join us now that they had finished dealing with an incident. Our Kendal escort had arrived, and again, thankfully, so had the sun.

A number of the firefighters, including a firewoman, dismounted from their machines and walked the last few miles into Kendal

Swasie meets his Kendal escort

alongside me. On entering Kendal the crews (except one firefighter, Ian Spate, who kindly remained with me to show me the way) remounted their machines and drove through the narrow streets to the nearby fire station. Ian and I meandered alongside a beautiful river on which a number of swans and their smaller cousins, ducks, swam to and fro in their constant search for aquatic tit bits. After passing through a narrow entry, we came out alongside the very impressive, Police, Fire and Ambulance buildings. As we passed the front of the police station I asked my brigade mentor, 'D'you fancy calling in to see the lads for a minute?' I was greeted with a blank, icy stare. 'Not particularly' replied Ian. Apparently (and sadly) the relationship between the police and fire there is not what one would describe as 'hot!' 'Oh come on, I'd like to say hello to the cloth', I persisted. Ian sighed and muttered, 'As you wish' and we both entered the foyer of the station. I was soon to learn the reason for Ian's lack of enthusiasm to call in at the Nick!

Once again I was to experience something I'd rather not believe. A young constable appeared, and on seeing the fully uniformed firefighter from next door and myself, with my Merseyside police cap proudly adorning my head, he sighed, placed his hands on his hips with his head leaning to one side, and grunted, 'Yeah?' I introduced myself and informed the officer of my arrival at Kendal and told him I just popped in to say hello to the lads. 'Yeah, well, what d'yer want me to do?' asked the identical replica of the Fort William ambassador to the Police Service. I spun my chair round and made for the door but as I was about to leave I turned to the young constable and snapped curtly, 'Young man, I want you to do precisely bugger all for me'. Ian and I left the open-mouthed detriment to the service and made for the fire station next door. Ian turned to me and shrugged his shoulders, 'See what I mean?' he said with complete justification.

The weather continued to be warm and sunny. I made my way to the canteen where I was joined by the station's ADO. I told him about the incident with the young bobby. The ADO did no more than to contact his counterpart, the Superintendent next door and within minutes the Super joined us for a cuppa at the table. Lo and behold, if the super wasn't an old Merseyside colleague of mine from days gone by. I emphasised that I didn't want anyone to get into trouble, but 'a little advice as to PR wouldn't go amiss' I quipped. 'Leave it with me Swasie, it'll be something more than a case of 'Advice Given' I can assure you', promised the not too pleased Superintendent.

At 6.00 a.m. that night White Watch came on duty. Then, after a press and photo shoot was completed I was asked to give a talk to a troop of little 'Rainbows' in the station canteen. This was a delightful task, as I loved to talk to the children. The little brownie rainbows sat there open-mouthed and enthralled as I related my adventures among all the animals and birds of prey in the Scottish Highlands. Again, as in Slamannan, their questions were highly amusing and innocently cheeky.

I befriended the watch's Leading Firefighter, Steve Wright, an ex-Falklands conflict veteran of 3 Para. We bonded immediately. We discussed the 1982 conflict and my wheelchair 'tab' across the same route he had taken across that unforgiving and inhospitable terrain during the battles of '82.

Mr John Wilmot, the Chief Executive from Lomax, unexpectedly arrived to take Grant and I to a local restaurant for dinner. His gesture was very much appreciated and the three of us left to have a wonderful meal and an extremely enjoyable evening. As usual, all good things eventually come to an end and finally, the thoughts of the comfortable warm bed, which awaited me back at the station, brought about the demise of our little social gathering. I thanked John for the warm, hospitable evening he had treated us to before retiring. John delivered us back to our 'digs' where I immediately made for the sanctuary of my warm bed to sleep the night away.

Day Twenty-one

Off to Lancaster today. Our warm and sunny day started at 9.15 a.m. with a two-machine escort through the streets of Kendal and out onto the open road toward our goal, which was 22 miles away. Things went well and the benevolent British motorists continued to stop and donate generously to our cause. After a couple of miles, our escort left us to return to base. I pushed on along the extremely busy A6 with my ever-protective Grant a short distance behind ensuring my safety. Thankfully I was enjoying the luxury of roads that were flat and level for a change, however, being blessed with such luxury was not to be a long lasting feature of my day's travels as I would still encounter numerous 'naughty' hills!

As I trundled on I received a number of calls on my mobile. The voices of my good friend, the well-known actor Derek Fowlds and his colleague, the lovely Tricia filled my earpiece. Both rang from the set of Heartbeat in Leeds during their mid-morning break from filming. The celebrity duo wished me well and promised to keep in touch as I plodded on down the country. Granada television then phoned to inform me that a news camera crew would be intercepting my travels 'some time within the next couple of days'. The ever faithful 'Fuji Films', another of my generous sponsors, also rang to tell me that they had dispatched a parcel of film for me which was now waiting for me at Lancaster. Fuji *always* ensured that my film supply *never* 'ran dry', *wherever* I was.

Eventually I saw a fire engine in the distance parked in a lay-by. As I approached the machine, the crew got out to greet me. Among the crew was a pretty young lady, Sue. All the lads greeted me with a warm, firm handshake. However, I had an additional 'perk'. I had the privilege of receiving a nice warm hug and a peck on the cheek from the beautiful Sue!

The crew was to be our new escort into Lancaster.

We moved off and the crew and I fell in behind the machine with Grant bringing up the rear. Our little 'motorcade' slowly meandered along as we continued to have our buckets generously 'topped up' by benevolent motorists and the ever-generous public. At one time we were joined by a number of children and their parents. I felt like the 'Pied Piper of Hamelin' as we made our way into the crowded and bustling town of Lancaster. As we entered the town a television camera crew appeared and started to film our progress. They stayed with us until our ultimate arrival at Lancaster Fire Station at 4.00 p.m. After being interviewed by T.V., Grant and I settled ourselves in at the station where I was handed my parcel from Fuji. We were well and truly *'film solvent'* again! I washed and changed then rang Chris and my daughter Jo to inform them of my safe arrival.

At 6.00 p.m. the night shift came on duty and Grant and I enjoyed a hearty meal of sausage, egg and chips (on a plate!) with the lads, courtesy of the night's cook, the Leading Firefighter. After tea, Jo rang to inform me that she had seen us on the television news. We later received a visit from Art and Tom from Lomax. Art handed me a newspaper, which featured our push, and proceeded to show everyone the photographs he had taken during the first part of our trek. As we all perused the pictures, Grant sat at a nearby table counting out the *large* amount of money we had accumulated.

I was summoned to the station telephone, as there was a call for me. My friend Peter Dann, a Sub Officer with the Merseyside Fire Brigade, rang to tell me that he would meet me on the A6 in the morning and accompany me for the next three days. This was great news and a considerable boost to my morale. Peter was an ardent fundraiser for the Fire Brigade Benevolent Fund and had accompanied me on many previous fundraising endeavours.

Eventually Art and Tom left and after a final supper time cup of tea, I updated my diary and turned in for the night. The 'jinx' manifested itself yet again – the crews were turned out twice during the night!

Chapter Fourteen
An Enjoyable Three Days of Fun and Banter

Day Twenty-two

UP AND READY for the day at 7.30 a.m. I enjoyed an early morning cuppa with the lads as they tidied up and checked their machines. They would be going off duty at 9.00 a.m. Grant was still 'unconscious' but he would have to move himself soon!

It was truly a strange feeling 'living' on fire stations again. I felt that there had been no interval (of nearly 35 years) since I had been an operational firefighter. The routine, the noises, banging, shouts, the smell, the cold and draughty stations, *all* these ingredients gave me the feeling that I was *still* a serving member of the Fire Service. Even when the 'bells went down' (i.e. the fire alarms sounded) during the night, I instinctively jumped up ready to 'turn out'! Had I been able-bodied, I felt quite confident that I could mount a machine and drive out to a shout without any trouble.

Although it was a grey morning, the clouds seemed to be high and it *was* dry. A bleary-eyed Grant appeared, muttering incoherently to himself about it being 'the crack of dawn'! He shuffled his way along making his way out to check the van and put our 'nighties' back on board. '*Good* morning Grant' said I, 'Uh. ----- !', he grunted with one of his Gaelic profanities which sounded very much like advice for me to call at the 'Foreign Office' – *forthwith*!

The day shift (Green Watch) paraded for duty at 9.00 a.m., then, after they had completed their vehicle and equipment checks we all sat down to a full breakfast of buttered toast and marmalade with a mug of tea accompaniment, followed by bacon, eggs and beans. After our morning gastronomic ritual we all rose from the trough and made our way outside to prepare for 'lift off'.

As we were about to set off, Granada TV arrived to film our departure. Our impressive motorcade this morning consisted of three fire engines, me, and finally our 'end-to-end' liveried van. What an impressive sight this was. I had an immense feeling of deep pride knowing I had been a member of, and was still *fiercely* loyal to and involved with, our highly professional emergency services. The sight of, and particularly *the reason* for our 'procession', brought a lump to my throat. I knew that Marje would be *so* proud of me.

As these sensitive and sentimental thoughts ran through my grieving mind, I could not prevent the tears from tumbling down my cheeks. Oh *how* I miss my Marje, my 'Child Bride' as I used to call her with affection. I took a deep breath and powered my chair away from the station and on to the highways and byways. After three miles, my escort left me. We all shook hands and said our goodbyes then our wonderful hosts turned around and made off back to their station.

I pushed on and now had a new incentive. The knowledge that my pal Peter Dann would be meeting me within the next few miles boosted my morale considerably. My strength and stamina powered me on along the busy A6. Suddenly I heard a shout from somewhere. I couldn't see who it was that was shouting, nor could I distinguish what was said. I carried on with my labours and pushed on through a set of traffic lights and continued through a busy shopping centre.

Suddenly I saw a large, stuffed sheep, which was mounted, on a castered trolley on the pavement at the roadside. I was absolutely fascinated by what I saw. It was a massive, *real* sheep! It was obviously advertising the woolshop it stood in front of. What a truly *golden* opportunity! I just could *not* resist this chance of a lifetime's photogenic gift. I mounted the pavement and positioned myself alongside the sheep. I placed my arms around its neck and gave it a cuddle and a big wet, passionate kiss on its lips, signalling for Grant to photograph the spectacle as I did so. My actions brought whistles and ribald banter from all that witnessed the scene. Motorists

Swasie and his 'new girlfriend', a stuffed sheep

sounded their horns as they passed. Everyone seemed highly amused at my antics. I intended to show *everyone* back home the picture, and tell them all about my new girlfriend!

Once again I heard shouting, this time I could *clearly* hear what was said. 'I always thought there was something funny about you Swasie, now I'm convinced!' I recognised the voice instantly. It was my Merseyside Fire Brigade pal from Wirral, Peter Dann. Peter then joined me and said, 'Hiya Ugly, I've come to join yer'! Pointing to the sheep he asked, 'Who's she?' A friend of Peter's had kindly driven him all the way out here to join me, what a decent guy to have driven him all that way. It was in fact Peter's shouts I heard earlier as they passed me before turning round to catch me up. I knew I would find the rest of the day's twenty something mile push easy going. Continual banter and quips eliminated the aches and pains of my numerous hill climbs. We trekked on until finally we arrived at the very impressive 'Fulwood House', the Headquarters of the Lancashire Fire Brigade.

On our arrival the Deputy Fire Chief, Mr Gerry O'Neil, gave us a very warm welcome. The 'Boss' then ensured that the three of us were adequately 'fed and watered' (in the Officers' mess). Mr O'Neil decreed that instead of spending the night at Preston Fire Station as arranged, we would spend the next two nights at the extremely prestigious and World renowned International Fire Services Training Centre at nearby Washington Hall.

This was a fantastic gesture, we would be staying almost at the 'Dorchester'! We were to be the *special guests* of the Commandant, ADO David Burton, another 'Officer and a Gentleman' of the service. Each of us was allocated our own en-suite room and also, I would have the additional privilege of being the *very* first occupant of the brand new 'special' suite for the disabled.

We then left the kind and generous Chief and went on to conclude the day's push at Preston. Pete and I then boarded the Lomax van and Grant drove us all back to Washington Hall. Appreciating my luxurious quarters, I decided to treat myself to the soothing relaxation of a (yet another) hot bath to enable the tiring results of the day's 23-mile push to evaporate from me.

Being as it was now Saturday night, it was decided that the three of us would 'dine' at a nearby pub.

We walked (I wheeled!) along to a local hostelry where we enjoyed a mouth watering steak dinner (I was a confirmed steakaholic!). After our meal we moved into the bar for a 'few drinks'. There, we met and joined a charming couple, Kevin McManus and his pretty wife Donna. During the rest of the evening, all (except me) consumed a fair amount of 'happy juice'. The evening's revelry went on until finally it was time to go 'home'. By the time Pete, Grant and I returned to our Washington Hall 'Four Star Hotel', I was the only one sober!

I wondered what tomorrow, Sunday, would be like with regard to traffic and collecting funds. I imagined that Preston would be deserted early on a Sunday morning when we started off.

Once inside the warm confines of my 'exclusive pad' however, such thoughts vanished. I decided to make myself a cup of tea then lay on the bed watching the last of the night's TV entertainment. Alas however, the 'Sandman' finally arrived and forced me to 'turn in'. I settled down between the sheets and was asleep in an instant.

Day Twenty-three

After my night's hibernation, I was up and ready for the day's activities at 7.00 a.m. on a warm, bright and sunny morning. I gave my mobile phone a boosting charge then set about 'rousing' the other two. I could hear both of them snoring loudly and banged on their doors. I shouted to each of them, informing them of the time and was again, (this time by Peter), advised in no uncertain terms to call at the proverbial '**Foreign Office**' – *forthwith*! Once the others were up and about, our dynamic little trio wandered around the vast training complex. Grant took numerous photographs of the train, aircraft, helicopter and other equally fascinating facilities that enhanced the establishment's training facilities. Finally, we boarded our van and drove to Preston Fire Station where we would start our day's push. Again we had breakfast with the lads and yet again we found we had taken our 'jinx' along with us, as the crews had to abandon their breakfast half way through when they were summoned to an incident.

After washing our dishes and making a fresh brew of tea for hot water to be added, Pete, Grant and I placed the crews' partly consumed breakfasts into a warm oven.

We set off for Chorely, passing through Standish en route. Today's push was only just over 20 miles so it was expected to be reasonably pleasant and easy. Time should pass quickly during the push with having Pete and his encouraging banter as company. Our Preston crews eventually caught up with us and kindly accompanied us for a mile or so. They were then relieved by another crew, who, in turn, were eventually relieved by a crew from Chorley. One member of our escort from Chorley was a 'scouser' from Kirkby called Paddy –

a typical Liverpool 'comedian' who enhanced our trek with his continual jokes and innuendos! The Chorley crew were a great bunch. They all dismounted from their machine to walk with Pete and I and audaciously collected donations from anyone they saw. The cash flowed and children joined us for most of our fun packed push each time we passed through a residential area.

When we reached Chorley we found to our complete surprise, that it was their annual festival day! Crowds of people were awaiting various processions and floats to travel through the town. Our arrival was greeted by applause and we were given generous donations for our buckets. As our own little 'procession' passed a local garage, the proprietor came out and handed a couple of most welcome bottles of iced coke to a hot and sweating Pete and I. Shortly after, two children ran up to us and gave Pete and I an ice cream. On seeing a couple of people in wheelchairs at the side of the road I went to them and greeted each with a handshake and a hug. The people gave generously as they awaited the arrival of *their own* festival floats, bands and majorettes. We had totally and *inadvertently* intruded into *their* festival. The festivities supported their town's own charities and

Swasie meets another 'Wheelchair Pilot' and his carer

many people were strategically placed with their collecting tins. Unfortunately, as many of the town's residents handed donations to us as we passed through, *some* did show resentment at what they no doubt interpreted as our audacity. Our happy progress was marred when one pompous, self important local 'jobs worth' approached Peter and rudely chastised him for accepting money from people when their own charities needed funds. Although I conceded that he had a point, I nevertheless informed him that being totally unaware of the day's festivities it was *purely* a coincidence that we were passing through his town during what was their annual charity fundraising festival day. The man would not be appeased. To evade the *certainty* of a 'not too friendly' response from Peter to his chastising tirade, I diplomatically pushed my chair between Pete and the obnoxious man to defuse the situation. I grabbed Peter's arm and pulled him away. I sarcastically informed the man that I would return along the whole length of the town and hand back all the loose change we had been given by the kind people of Chorley, once I had identified them! This time, it was the 'Woolyback' from Chorley who advised Peter and I – to call at the proverbial 'Foreign Office'! He even suggested to us both where we could 'stick our cash'! I had the distinct impression that this particular miserable individual was not very impressed by our visit to his town!

Adamantly refusing to neither visit the 'Foreign Office' n*or* deposit our donations where the unfriendly man had suggested, Peter and I carried on through the otherwise *very* friendly town. As we made our way along we were cheered by a group of pretty little majorettes, resplendent in their bright blue, white and gold uniforms as they smartly marked time in unison to the whistle and flute band. We reached Chorley Fire Station and were joined by Shirley Chisnall, Editor of the *Police and Fire News*. Her photographer Simon accompanied her. After a welcome cup of tea Shirley interviewed me and photographs were taken to illustrate a forthcoming feature regarding the 'end-to-end' push in the *Fire News*.

Finally, when all was concluded, Grant drove us back to Washington Hall for our final night there. We washed and changed and again made for the local hostelry to dine. This time our meal was one of lamb and chips. We met an off duty Lancs County policewoman and her boyfriend. Unfortunately, the couple smoked and once the offensive little white sticks were produced and lit I decided it was time for me to beat a hasty retreat. Smoking and I are *totally* incompatible and acceptance of this habit non-negotiable. I find this habit to be grossly offensive and I will not tolerate the risk of breathing in such filth. I left the little throng and returned to my room at Washington Hall. I didn't need to explain my absence to the amused Pete and Grant, as they were fully aware of my sentiments regarding the dreaded weed.

Chapter Fifteen
A Welcome En-Route Visit by 'Matron' and my Family

Day Twenty-four

AT 7.00 A.M. I was up like a lark and all set for the day, I left my room and wandered along the corridor to Peter's 'House'. Grant joined us soon afterwards. The three of us had a cup of tea then returned to clear our rooms before packing our gear aboard the van ready for the drive to the day's starting point.

Grant was to be our only escort from the start and Peter and I set off making for Wigan. The weather was again kind with just a slight breeze and sunny skies, however, there were streaks of red showing in the morning heavens! 'Red sky in the morning...'?

I pushed on and on and every now and again a kindly motorist would stop to hand us something for our bucket. The push was receiving enormous amounts of media coverage and the continual publicity generated the required interest which, in turn, resulted in financial benevolence as we made our way steadily southwards down the country. At first the day's donations were sparse, but as the morning's local news bulletins carried our story and announced our presence in the area they increased. After pushing for 15 miles or so we were due to rendezvous with our Greater Manchester escort which would take us on to Wigan Fire Station where we would have our 'tea and toast'.

However, as the saying goes, 'The best made plans.....!' *Somehow*, we missed our escort. Apparently the machine had left the station to look for us but failed to find the illusive man in the wheelchair and his companions! Eventually, after sticking to our *designated* route,

Grant's navigation finally took us to our intended refuge where we met the lads and their Station Commander. The Commander, a heavily built Station Officer, was one hell of a character. It was *immediately* apparent that this big man was not only an extremely popular boss, but was also highly respected by his subordinates. His manner oozed warm, friendly hospitality and he made sure we, his temporary guests, wanted for nothing. He even made the tea himself. As we sat there devouring our thick doorsteps of buttered toast and slurping our tea, the station's (very beautiful) cook arrived. Boy, she was a *stunner*! I watched as Pete and Grant patted their hair and '*tried*' to make themselves look presentable and attractive. (I should cocoa!) The young lady bid us all good morning and made for the kitchens to begin her day's chores. She never even gave my two companion 'Casanovas' a second glance! The machine, which was meant to be our escort, then arrived back at the station. The surprised driver, on seeing us, exclaimed, 'I've just been out looking for you, which way did you come?'

The driver took some raucous stick from his colleagues, especially the Station Officer who questioned his topographical skills by asking his embarrassed subordinate, 'What the hell are you on about Duffy? There's only one main road into here', and rolling his eyes to the ceiling he gasped, 'Phew! – Bloody drivers – yer just can't get the staff nowadays'. The banter continued, mainly directed at the hapless driver until, eventually we left, with our escort, to make our way to distant Newton Le-Willows where we would rendezvous with our Merseyside escort.

After a further hour's pushing I received a call on my mobile. It was my son Ron who informed me that Chris was driving out to meet me, bringing him, his daughter Sophie and my daughter Jo with her. They expected to be with me shortly. This was great news. I looked forward to seeing them all, as I had been visually incommunicado from my family for 24 days, nearly a whole month! Again, the news did wonders for my strength and stamina. Eventually, after continually scrutinising the oncoming traffic I finally spotted Chris's

grey Trooper approaching. As she passed she flashed her headlights
and all aboard waved. Chris gesticulated to indicate she would turn
around and join us. She tagged on to the end of our little procession
and a short distance further along I saw our Cheshire (Warrington)
escort parked in a lay-by awaiting our arrival. We all pulled into the
lay-by astern of the Warrington machine and I greeted my family with
warm emotion. Again, my deep, intense pride brought a lump to my
throat as Jo, Chris and Ronnie hugged me and congratulated me on
my physically demanding trek so far. Grant and some of the others
took photographs of the impressive line up of vehicles with our little
group standing alongside them. Again, I had a vivid vision of my
Marje, her face glowing with pure unadulterated pride at what *her*
husband and her family were bringing about and achieving, in her
name.

Chris decided she would join the 'motorcade' and follow us all to
Warrington. Ronnie and Jo elected to walk alongside their dad and
his pal Pete Dann.

Matron joins the escort

Eventually our happy little throng wandered onto the car park and stopped outside the supermarket next to 'Burger King'. There, the sight of the fire engine and our little group with the flagged wheelchair, the same chair that was the subject of so much media attention, instantly drew lots of attention. Once the management was aware of our presence, one of the major stores sent out a tray of cold drinks for our thirsty group.

After half an hour we left this financially beneficial venue with our buckets brimming. We waved goodbye to the many donors and their fascinated children. During our brief stay, the fire crew had kindly allowed many of the children the opportunity to climb aboard the 'big red fire engine'.

We plodded on until we reached our day's final destination, Warrington Fire Station. I rolled across the concrete apron and round to the rear of the big building. The station's Commander ushered us all to the canteen where we were all furnished with a cup of tea. I sat with my family chatting until, sadly, it was time for them to leave. They were *also* taking Pete back with them at the conclusion of his three-day walk with me, returning him home to the Wirral. My previous feelings of elation now turned into depression as I saw Chris's Trooper leave the station and vanish out of sight. I had no idea when I would be seeing them all again. However, the thought that I was now *halfway* through my anticipated 44-day push did help a little.

Grant obviously realised how I must be feeling and he immediately rectified the situation when he deliberately snapped, 'Hey! What's up with *your* gob?' at the same time ensuring that everyone present heard. His uncomplimentary rhetoric worked and I immediately snapped out of my lethargy and went off to wash and change. It would soon be time for us to sit down with the lads for dinner. After dinner Grant wandered off out to a nearby pub for a pint while I rang Chris then went off to bed. Yet another day completed, and yet another day towards my *journey's* end – at *Land's* End.

Chapter Sixteen
Chief Fire Officer's Presentation

Day Twenty-five

DURING THE NIGHT, the bells went down twice, sending the crews out to a fire and a traffic accident. The latter incident prevented them resuming their slumbers. The 'Jinx' again!

Due to the noise and the 'hive of activity' that prevailed, I got up and had a brew with the lads downstairs. Grant slept through all and didn't join us until the 'big finger was nearly on twelve and the little finger was on eight'! His eyes looked like the proverbial – '..... holes in snow'! 'I see you had a good time last night then Grant?' I asked. My question was met with a cold, bleary-eyed stare, accompanied by a grunt.

I had intended to make an early start today as my push would be over *30 miles*. However, first I had an appointment at the studios of 'Wire FM Radio'. I just had a couple of rounds of toast and a mug of tea before I made my way to the studio at 8.30 a.m. Once my interview was concluded I set off with Grant for far away Crewe.

We were to call at Winsford Fire Station en route where we would meet the Chief Fire Officer of Cheshire Fire Brigade, Mr McGirk. As I left the studio I was met by a group of small children and their teachers.

Pictures were taken of us all then I left on my lengthy trek. Shortly after Grant and I set off from the studio I was delighted to see our Warrington crew come to escort us. The lads jumped out and walked alongside me. This was great, I enjoyed the crews' company during my pushes; their banter and conversation was a continual tonic. I

Swasie and children outside 'Wire Radio'

missed Peter Dann already. The trouble about someone joining the push, after being used to 'flying solo', is that you start to get used to the company of a close friend and then it is hard when that close friend departs and you are on your own again.

My Warrington escort eventually left me and I carried on for some miles, still collecting cash! Eventually a machine from Stockton Heath met me. They stayed with me for a few miles before we pulled onto a transport café lorry park to 'change escorts'. My new Winsford escort was already there waiting for me. The lady proprietor of the establishment, wondering why two fire engines were parked outside her café, came out to investigate. On learning the reason for our presence she returned inside, shortly to reappear with a tray of drinks, sandwiches and a £20 note for the bucket. She was followed by a number of her lorry driver customers who also gave generously. We drank our fruit drinks and continued on towards Winsford, 'shedding' our previous escort.

My route today included some long and 'naughty' hills to Northwich and Winsford. I could certainly do without these on such a long haul. However, as always, the company of the crew was a tonic and a morale booster. Typical service banter and innuendo prevailed which helped to consume distance and quickly pass away the time.

Cheshire Fire Brigade Chief greets Swasie

We arrived at Winsford where I was pleasantly surprised when I was greeted by Miss Jan Heyes, the Clatterbridge Cancer Fund Co-ordinator. Jan joined us all while we rested over yet another cup of tea in the station canteen. A Station Officer entered the room and asked us all to accompany him to the Administration block next door, where Cheshire's Fire Chief personally greeted us all warmly. Mr McGirk and his entourage of senior officers congratulated me on my marathon push and thanked me for my regular, ongoing assistance to the Fire Services National Benevolent Fund. The Chief then kindly presented me with a pair of cufflinks bearing his Brigade's crest and a souvenir moneybox in the shape of a fire engine.

When our little 'ceremony' was concluded, Grant and I left our kind hosts and made our way to Crewe Fire Station where we would be staying overnight. I had yet another pleasant surprise when Chris arrived for an hour's visit after tea. I also received a telehone call from Merseyside Chief Constable, Mr Norman Bettison, who wished me well on my travels.

Grant, Chris and I set about counting and bagging the day's cash collection. Our efforts revealed the amazing sum of our day's endeavours was over £700. The day's gruelling push had totalled 31 miles. Chris left to return home at 10.00 p.m. and as soon as she left I made straight for my bed and soon became oblivious to any further proceedings on the station due to my deep slumbers. The 'bells went down' at 3.30 a.m. when the crews were summoned to a house fire. I turned over and resumed my pleasant nocturnal anaesthesia.

Day Twenty-six

I rose from my pit at 6.00 a.m., updated my diary to ensure accurate chronology then washed and dressed before making for the canteen for an early morning mug of hot, sweet tea. Grant joined me after he had checked the van and completed his various bits of paper work. The weather today was warm and sunny (which would hopefully enhance my tan!).

After a substantial 'traditional' Brigade breakfast we set off with a two-machine escort through the already busy town of Crewe. From the very start the money started to roll in. The benevolent motorists and lorry drivers caused a traffic jam (in both directions) as we made our way out of town. This again illustrated the popularity of the fire service and the esteem in which it is held. Once out of town the two-machine escort left us. However, a couple of off-duty firefighters from Crewe joined us in a vehicle that was 'off the run'. Instead of going home from night duty, the kindly duo volunteered to escort us all the way to our next stopover, the retained fire station at Market Drayton. However, this little town was a long way off yet. Pete, one of the Crewe firefighters left his pal at the wheel to join me out on the road. The considerate Pete would walk alongside me for the duration of the day's push, tirelessly collecting cash donations from the generous public as he did so.

We stopped for a refreshment break at the very old and well-known town of Nantwich. We were joined here by Chris, my mentor, who was this day working nearby at her duties as a professional Store Detective. Her job takes her all over the Northwest. Our little group stopped for a break in the little town's centre, savouring the sheer delight of iced drinks in the warm sunshine. The town's generosity manifested itself when numerous, interested and inquisitive locals gathered round to talk to us and 'feed' our buckets. After quenching my insatiable thirst and replacing lost body fluid we continued on. Chris accompanied us as far as the beautiful and tranquil village of Audlem. Here we again stopped for a break and to admire the beautiful little village. The only sound was of jackdaws squawking loudly as they surveyed us from the safety of their nests high above in the chimney pots, roofs and nearby trees. Chris 'Matron' could not resist the temptation to photograph this beautiful rural utopia before leaving us once again.

After a further couple of miles a reporter and photographer from the *Shropshire Advertiser* intercepted us. I was subsequently interviewed whilst I was rolling. During this time, a police car driven by Policewoman Liz Downes also joined us. Liz very kindly drove ahead at each major junction where she would alight from her vehicle and perform 'point duty' to ensure our safe passage. Her *much* appreciated company and kind assistance were invaluable and saved us a lot of time. I considered the sight of this 'joint' escort by *two* of the main emergency services would certainly be a *massive* boost to public relations. I certainly hoped to see and be accompanied by the police *many* more times during my lengthy push.

Finally we reached the unmanned retained fire station at Market Drayton just as the clouds gathered to welcome us with a hefty downpour! A reporter and cameraman arrived at the same time from the *Market Drayton Gazette* and, not to be thwarted by inclement weather, photographs were taken. One of the retained firefighters, Mark, arrived to unlock the door and let us all into the station where, getting his priorities right, his *first* duty was to furnish us all with a cup of tea! I was eager to get out of my wet clothes as I was now rapidly getting cold.

After changing into a warm and dry set of clothes I was quite happy to be interviewed by the press. When all was done and Grant

Police and Fire photo shoot at (wet) Market Drayton

had finished bringing in our sleeping bags and sorted where we would be sleeping, our kind policewoman, Liz, pulled another much appreciated 'rabbit out of the hat'. She took Grant and I along to the nearby Crown Hotel. There, she introduced us to Dennis and Annie, the hotel's proprietor licensees. We all sat in the warm, hospitable confines of the well-furnished lounge and chatted over a drink. Liz briefed the two 'mine hosts' as to my fundraising push and arranged for us to dine there later in the evening. Liz was an absolute gem and credit to her force. She certainly knew how to enhance police and public relations. Subsequently, Grant and I enjoyed a wonderful dinner (our hosts, allowing us both a *very* generous discount). Our more than generous hosts also donated £20 to our charity.

After returning to the station, Grant and I discovered that tonight was the station's drill night. At the conclusion of the night's training, the 'troops' gathered in the station club where everybody enjoyed numerous pints of 'Happy juice', including Grant, who *never* missed a chance to partake! ADO, Mike Ablitt attended the evening's gathering to welcome Grant and I. During the latter part of the evening's 'festivities' he organised a collection amongst his men, which eventually resulted with him proudly presenting me with the princely sum of £85.

Eventually, this very eventful day drew to a close. The place was tidied and after all the glasses were cleared away, everyone made their way home. Once again silence reigned. In no time at all Grant and I were fast asleep, burrowed deep down inside our warm sleeping bags *on the floor*!

Chapter Seventeen
The Mayoral Cortina

Day Twenty-seven

AFTER A RESTLESS night I finally decided to get up at 7.00 a.m. I slid out of my bag to get my circulation going then made a mug of tea and a couple of rounds of toast. I didn't disturb Grant, as there was no hurry for him to be up and about at this time of the morning. Today's push would be only a short distance of approximately 20 miles which was to take us as far as the Shropshire town of Wellington. The town had a 'full time' fire station which would ensure that tonight we would have a bed to sleep in. I sat my aching frame at the table and ate my buttered toast, washing it down with my tea. I read an old magazine whilst having to listen to Grant's rendition of the 1812 overture via his loud and thunderous snoring. I switched the television on intending to turn the volume up high to drown Grant's snores. However, I thought better of this and allowed his slumbers to continue unabated. I kept the volume down very low instead as I watched the early morning news. No matter *what* major world crisis would be featured, one thing *was* certain, my pal Grant would be utterly and totally oblivious to it!

I sat there pensively, thinking about my 'exclusive' and adventurous push. There is no doubt that I *had* thoroughly enjoyed it so far and wouldn't have missed such an opportunistic 'first' for the world. When I reflected on this, my personal endeavour, the good times tended to pale the bad ones into insignificance. By and large the whole fundraising enterprise had, to date, been a resounding success. Each day had furnished an individual 'adventure' of one sort or another and not forgetting the fact that we had collected a vast amount of money for my chosen charities. I was *definitely* pleased!

Eventually the bundle on the floor stirred, grunted and *actually* moved! I asked the muttering Scot if he would like a cup of tea. Grant stirred again and muttered, 'Grrmnnnobllmnmnm-thanoo'! I interpreted this to be an affirmative response and duly handed a mug of tea to my still, semi-conscious pal! As Grant slurped his tea and rambled on incoherently I proceeded to pedantically update my diary as to my endeavours and events.

The weather looked as though it was going to be kind again. The bright morning sun was already sending its warm shafts of light in through the big windows after I had drawn the curtains wide. A shaft of light '*in*appropriately' shone down to highlight the figure on the floor, no doubt attempting to portray Grant as m*y* guardian angel...in my dreams!

Grant put his arm across his eyes to shield them from the bright sun 'Grrrachano-chanoo the Bloody sun!' he grunted. He was obviously looking forward to his sprightly new day with relish. The next thing I expected him to do was spring forth from his sleeping bag like a Jack in the Box then sing and dance his way, *pirouetting*, across the room and along to the shower!

Just as we were about to set off this morning Liz, the policewoman, arrived to walk through the town with us. The sight of her in her high visibility, yellow jacket would help our cause considerably as we made our way up and out of town. Peter the retained firefighter then arrived, having forfeited some of his 'earning' time by absenting himself from his business so that he could accompany us for part of today's trek in the fire station's Land Rover. *What* a bloody good gesture, I thought. As we left the town, Liz took her leave of us to resume her usual duties. Grant and I thanked her profusely and I had the additional 'perk' of kissing her goodbye as we parted company. Peter would selflessly stay with us, leading all the way to the point where we met our Wellington escort. After such a beautiful start to the day, the rain returned with a vengeance and I received another soaking. I found the rain to be refreshing as I powered myself on through what was an otherwise warm day.

As I pushed along and up another hill I saw the familiar sight of a fire engine parked in a lay-by just over the brow. I had now reached the outskirts of Wellington. Time (and the rain) had passed quickly today and I still felt quite fresh. The Wellington crew of Blue Watch (my old watch) stood alongside their machine and gave me a much appreciated applause of encouragement as I approached them. Peter then turned around and waved farewell as he passed, flashing his blue light and sounding his two-tone horns in salute. He soon disappeared into the spray of the still wet roads, making his way back to Market Drayton. His truly selfless gesture truly highlights the close, warm bond, of the '*brotherhood*', which is so unique and special to members of the emergency services wherever they may be.

I continued along with members of my new crew walking alongside me. Donations were now non-existent, having been eliminated during the recent spell of inclement weather. However, I *was* enjoying the company of my escort and in no time we arrived at

Wellington escort meets Swasie

Wellington Fire Station. As usual, Grant and I experienced the traditional warm welcome. In no time the two of us were upstairs in the canteen drinking tea and meeting everyone on the station.

Blue Watch was subsequently replaced by Red Watch and, after a nice hot dinner of curried beef and rice, I retired to my welcome bed. I received calls from Jo and Chris before placing my phone on charge and sinking into the depths of slumbering oblivion.

Day Twenty-eight

The day started well: bright, warm and sunny. There didn't appear to be a cloud in sight. This morning I would be propelling my trusty chair all the way to Bridgnorth Fire Station for tonight's overnight stay.

At the moment I was about to push away from Wellington Fire Station with Grant and my fire engine escort, I was suddenly summoned to the station watch room as there was a telephone call for me. The Mayor of Wellington's secretary was on the phone, calling from the Town Hall. The lady asked if I would await the arrival of the town's Mayor, Councillor Gary Davies, who specifically wished to meet me and give me an official send off from Wellington. I informed the lady that not only would I be *delighted* to await the Mayor's arrival but I also deemed it an absolute *honour and privilege* for His Worship to take such trouble.

I returned outside to my 'gang' and called a halt to proceedings, informing all of the impending arrival of the town's Mayor. Panic set in as hasty arrangements were made for the Brigade photographer to attend and officially record the formal proceedings for posterity.

Within a *very* short time, the photographer arrived (thankfully before the Mayor) and immediately and pedantically set about getting us all into the 'correct' position for his photoshoot. He fussed about, making sure this was right and that was right; that we were facing the sun and the machines and the fire station would be strategically placed in the background for his pictures. Once he was satisfied that all *was* okay, the meticulous, budding 'David Bailey' finally set up his tripod, on to which he mounted and secured his camera. Eventually, all was now ready to record the official Mayoral 'send off' for the Brigade record books. We all stood (and I sat) waiting for the big, black shiny Mayoral limousine with its crested pennant flying from the bonnet, to glide silently to a stop before us. Then, the immaculately uniformed chauffeur would alight, open the door and smartly salute the red-robed Mayor with his gold chain of office glittering in the morning sunlight, while he stepped out to perform his little ceremony.

Suddenly a battered, old, white and rusty, mark two Ford Cortina drove onto the forecourt of the station, coughing and spluttering and belching clouds of blue smoke. As the driver parked his vehicle someone shouted angrily to him, 'Hey, get that bloody shed the hell out of here before the Mayor arrives'!

Either totally ignoring, or not having heard the irate instruction, the Cortina's driver got out of the vehicle and walked towards us. As he did so he reached into the pocket of his crumpled white jacket. To my surprise he then retrieved a thick, gold, crested chain of office, and placed it around his shoulders.

His Worship The Mayor had arrived!

The fascinating scenario of his arrival was totally deceptive. Once I met the Mayor I *very* soon realised what a thorough gentleman he was. First, he handed me an extremely generous and substantial donation for my charity, then went on at length to congratulate me, *and all those present*, for the excellent work we were doing in the name of charity. He expressed his deep pride in the town's fire service and stated that he would make sure the whole of Wellington would be made aware of today's proceedings via the town's media.

His Worship then kindly obliged the Brigade's 'David Bailey' and posed with us while the photographer took numerous pictures to ensure a pictorial record of the event was obtained for posterity.

Finally, when all was concluded the kindly Mayor thanked us all once more for what we were doing then bade us goodbye. I then set off into the wide blue yonder towards distant Bridgnorth; the shiny, red fire engine ahead of me and Grant following on behind. The other immaculate machine was left to 'guard' the station.

Although I had at first been amused by the Mayor's arrival, the *most* important thing was that the he had kindly appeared and honoured the station with a visit. The proceedings were gratefully enhanced and graced by his presence.

I was *extremely* proud and grateful at having had the privilege to meet such a *thoroughly* kind and honourable gentleman who is undoubtedly a true son of the warm, hospitable town of Wellington.

Our little procession snaked its way along, now and again receiving the occasional donation from a passing motorist or an avid gardner tending their blooms or pottering amongst their vegetables. This again illustrated the true value of *regular* publicity coverage by the media. By now, Wellington had disappeared far behind us over the horizon and was now only a fond, but permanently treasured memory. After another few miles, our escorting machine returned to its station leaving Grant and I to continue alone. At this point there was a long, one and a half mile hill to negotiate! The hard, slow push to the top took me well over half an hour. Finally, sweating and grunting, I reached my goal then gratefully savoured the comfort of a slight descent beyond the brow, at the same time enjoying a beautiful panoramic view of the countryside. As I pushed on, I was met by a fire tender from Bridgnorth, driven by Dave 'Bish' Bishop. Dave, a retained firefighter then escorted us the whole way to Bridgnorth Fire Station.

As we entered the quaint old town and negotiated its narrow and extremely steep, arm bursting hilly streets, a lady stepped out in front of me. The lady handed me a donation for my bucket and went on to inform me that her daughter owned a little restaurant in the town. Grant and I were cordially invited to join them both there for dinner later. I was handed a slip of paper bearing her daughter's telephone number and 'instructed' to ring and confirm our attendance. The meal would be with the compliments of her and her

Escort change; Wellington to Bridgnorth

daughter Linda. I thanked the lady for her generous offer, assuring her that we deemed it an honour to join them. I pushed on and rang Linda to 'book' our table as requested!

We arrived at the station and Bish did the honours by ensuring that Grant and I were quickly slurping from a nice hot mug of tea. We were joined shortly after our arrival by the tall, distinguished and familiar figure of ADO Mike Ablitt, our previously warm and generous host at Market Drayton. Later on in the evening, a smartened up duo in the form of Grant and I enjoyed a wonderful three-course meal, courtesy of our lady hosts Jean and Linda.

Even as we dined, I continually received donations from others who were dining out at the establishment. Again, our publicity had preceded our arrival at the ancient town. Bridgnorth is indeed a town of character. Sitting in the centre of the beautiful Severn Valley, the town is a mecca for antique seekers and souvenir hunters. The nearby terminus of the Severn Valley railway is a must for steam buffs. The town also boasts a beautiful, clean, slow flowing river where fishermen can test their skills as they sit and enjoy the peaceful tranquillity from its scenic banks as the river peacefully and silently meanders by.

At the conclusion of our more than adequate meal, our hosts adamantly refused to hear of us paying for such wonderful mouth-watering cuisine – end of story! We sincerely thanked both ladies for their kind generosity. The benevolent two informed me that they would be at the fire station in the morning to see us off on our journey to Kidderminster. I appreciated this and looked forward to seeing them both again in the morning.

Leaving the restaurant, Grant suggested that we wander around town before turning in for the night. We did a bit of 'exploring' and window-shopping as we walked among the evening's revellers. As we passed the pubs along the high street, Grant started to get the smell of 'the Barmaid's apron'. The alcoholic aroma drifting out from the confines of many taverns was like a magnet to my pal. Grant decided to visit a couple of these establishments for a 'pint or two' while I made my way 'home'. I felt awkward not staying with him as I am sure he would have appreciated the company during his 'induced anaesthetical' wanderings. However, due to my views on smoke-logged pubs and clubs, I refrained and pushed myself back to the station thinking of the forthcoming push to Kidderminster and wondering what adventures tomorrow's trek would bring.

Eventually I reached my sanctuary for the night where I quickly climbed into the confines of my waiting sleeping bag to savour the oblivion of a night's sleep on the floor of the station. Although it was a little uncomfortable at first, I soon settled down and was overcome by the welcome anaesthesia of slumber.

I never heard Grant's eventual arrival at the conclusion of his nocturnal 'tour of the town'!

Chapter Eighteen
Discovering a Mole in the Road

Day Twenty-nine

AFTER A QUIET night, with no turnouts for the lads, I awoke to the sounds of traffic passing by outside the station (and Grant's eternal snoring!). As the curtains were drawn there was hardly any light but I could just about see the station wall clock which told me that it was only 5.55 a.m. I decided to remain where I was for another hour or so. Try as I may, I could not get back to sleep. I lay on the hard floor tossing and turning – and cursing!

In the end I couldn't stand my uncomfortable, rock-hard 'bed' any longer and got up to wash, make a brew and forage among the cupboards to find something to eat. I found some cheese and biscuits and a packet of crisps. I sat in the small kitchen munching away until I had satisfied my appetite and finished my mug of tea. I wandered into the appliance room and looked over the machine and its equipment. I found that most of the firefighting gear and BA (Breathing Apparatus) equipment was still basically familiar to me, although there were many exceptions and improvements due to advancing technology. The ambience and smell of the equipment, the machines, and the fire kit brought my days as a firefighter back to me. I felt as though I was 'back in the job'. I enjoyed the 'espirite de corps' of the service and realised how much I actually missed my old Brigade comrades and the excitement of attending various, many dangerous, incidents during those distant days gone by.

The sound of cups rattling snapped me out of my mental firefighting reminiscences of long ago – Grant was up and about! I returned to the kitchen and joined him over another brew of tea.

As usual Grant was the absolute epitome of lengthy, early morning conversation and chatter! I was greeted with the usual barely audible grunt, 'Hi Swas'! Grant at first gives the impression of being miserable but in actual fact his character is deceiving and he is quite the opposite. Although a quiet and reserved chap he actually possesses one hell of a dry sense of humour and he is also blessed with a very quick wit.

In the two weeks he had been with me he had become very popular with the lads of the brigades we had stayed with. I liked him and enjoyed his company *very* much. Having at first missed Art, I now didn't want to lose Grant. Sadly, I only had one more day with him. Not once did I ever have cause to criticise Grant's continual care for my welfare during the whole time we were together. I could 'take for *grant*ed' my continual supply of drinks, cold *or* hot, (depending on what he considered appropriate) refreshments and food while I was on the 'hoof' (wheel!). With all respect to Art, the thought of Grant's impending departure saddened me greatly. Although both were *highly* efficient at looking after my welfare, as well as being my close friends, I prefer to keep secret *whom* I would prefer as my 'minder'!

At 8.00 a.m. ADO Mike Ablitt breezed into the station and informed us that he had managed to recruit some retained volunteers so that he and his crews could escort us to the edge of town with two machines as we set off for Kidderminster. True to their word, Jean and Linda, our previous evening's hosts, arrived. The kind and considerate ladies brought a parcel of sandwiches and pies to ensure we wouldn't go hungry during our day's forthcoming push. What a fantastic gesture.

When all was ready and we were about to set off, the local press arrived to chronicle and photograph our departure. A number of children gathered with their parents to wave us off as they were being escorted to school. To enhance the scene, the sun shone brightly as it rose into the morning sky and we were treated to the added bonus of the police joining us to lead the way. The day was starting well. There was one final surprise to 'put the icing on the cake'!

Police and Fire escort leaving Bridgnorth

ADO Ablitt formally presented me with a memorial plate together with a cheque for my bucket from him and his men. He then presented Grant with a memorial plate to mark the occasion of our visit. This surprise gesture was very much appreciated by the both of us and would remain a treasured memory, as would the unforgettably hospitable efforts of ADO Ablitt.

We made our way with our very impressive police and fire escort through the town, receiving many generous donations as we progressed. Our lengthy procession meandered on to raucous applause and waves from the town's people. I rang my brother Tom and, knowing how fond he is of this lovely town, I knew he would be extremely envious of my presence here. He and his wife Maureen are frequent visitors and regularly spend their holidays at this pleasant venue. My brother's passionate love affair with Bridgnorth began during the time he was stationed here with the RAF half a century ago. Tom could clearly hear the cheers of the crowd over the phone.

Our escort drew ahead and stopped their vehicles as we reached the edge of town. The crew dismounted from the machine. The 'Boss' formed the two crews into a straight line at the roadside. The ADO stood in front of his crew and as I drew level he brought his men to attention.

As I passed them I was given a final accolade when the ADO gave the command, 'Salute'. The sight of him and his men, lined up at the roadside with their machines, formally saluting as I passed, was an extremely moving sight, and a privilege I shall *never* forget. As I was wearing a cap, I formally acknowledged by returning the salute. Passing motorists were so impressed they acknowledged by sounding their horns and some even stopped to donate cash to our fund. I pushed on, alone now, and Grant rang my mobile to say how 'gobsmacked' he was to have witnessed such a spectacle!

Whilst making my way along through the beautiful countryside, I heard the accompanying sounds of birds singing, skylarks twittering and the buzz of grasshoppers amongst the long grass at the roadside. The cloudless blue sky was etched with vivid white 'chalk' marks from highflying jets as they conveyed their human cargoes off to distant continents. As I pushed along, savouring my feelings of utter utopia, the hot sun beat down adding to my now adequate tan. Now and again a motorist would stop to contribute to my bucket and bring me back to reality. Whilst I was enjoying the symphonic anaesthesia of Mother Nature's overtures, I saw something in the centre of the road ahead of me. A little furry creature had obviously wandered out from the protection of the roadside foliage exposing himself to the risk of the dangers of predation or passing traffic as he made his way out onto the highway.

As I got nearer, I saw that it was a little mole. I thought it was dead but as I looked closer and prodded it with my finger the little rodent moved. I grabbed the minute bundle of fur and held him aloft to show Grant. He jumped out of the van, camera in hand and took a couple of pictures of the sightless little creature. I said to Grant, 'I was lucky there Grant, I very nearly fell into a 'mole' in the road'!

Concerned for the safety of my new miniature friend I moved to the side of the road and placed him over the hedge into an adjacent field of long grass.

We proceeded on past fields of maturing fruit and vegetables and then, although the sky was devoid of cloud, I suddenly heard 'thunder'. The sound persisted and got louder. I looked into the field alongside me. I was treated to another amazing spectacle. A herd of inquisitive young bullocks were *galloping* towards me. The inquisitive regiment of black and white members of the Taurus infantry suddenly stopped ten yards from the fence. At first they stood mesmerised, eyeing the strange object in the wheelchair. As I '*mooved*' on, the potential oxo cubes followed at a discreet distance trying to figure out what on earth it was they were looking at. I was highly amused at witnessing such an unusual sight; unfortunately Grant didn't photograph the incident.

More and more miles rolled by beneath my wheels and casters then I saw two fire engines ahead, parked in a lay-by with their crews lying on a grass verge enjoying the sun. My Kidderminster escort awaited me! I went to the lads and introduced Grant and myself to them. One of them went to his machine then returned to hand us both a bottle of chilled water. As I was guzzling the contents of my bottle, my mobile phone rang. I received a call from a lifelong friend back home, Derek Tinsley, wishing me well and telling me he was monitoring my progress via the news. After a brief rest and my thirst satisfied, we moved off and, as usual, the lads walked with me. Donations continued to flow and we all eventually arrived at Kidderminster Fire Station after a lengthy trek. I wheeled myself around to the rear of the station past the 'oldest tree' in the town next to the town's equally oldest building, a stone tower. I could hear the soothing sound of rushing water from the river as it flowed past the station. I sat there in the sunshine while Grant parked his vehicle and the machines were returned to their bays inside the appliance room.

After we were settled in and shown our bunks, the shift concluded its day's tour of duty at 6.00 p.m. The off-going Watch Commander, Station Officer David Williams, took Grant and I to his home where we enjoyed a splendid dinner with him and his charming wife Sally Ann and their equally charming daughter Laura.

After dinner, Dave returned Grant and I to the station. One of the night shift crews took us on a wander around the town, collecting money. Their machine followed behind as it was 'on the run' and must be accessible should they get a 'shout'. We visited a bingo hall, two clubs and a venue hosting a number of civic dignitaries who were attending a dinner-dance. I was afforded the pleasure of meeting not only the Mayor and Mayoress of Kidderminster, but also fellow Mayors and their ladies from neighbouring towns, all of whom unhesitatingly and generously filled our buckets.

The Mayor of Kidderminster informed me that tomorrow, his town would be holding their annual carnival festival. His Worship kindly asked me if I would lead the carnival's large procession through the town during the afternoon's ceremonial festivities. I was *absolutely* delighted at such an honour and readily accepted such a prestigious privilege.

At the conclusion of the night's 'collecting patrol' our subsequent return to the station revealed we had collected a very substantial sum of money. After a cup of tea one of the firefighters asked me if I would sign one of my vests for him to keep. I was more than happy to oblige and immediately supplied him with a clean and duly autographed vest. After this I went straight off to bed, as I would be pushing for long periods and up many steep hills tomorrow, both through the town with the festival, as well as my lengthy push to Worcester.

Chapter Nineteen
Art's Return

Day Thirty

I GOT UP early this morning to make sure everything was sorted for today's activities and lengthy push. I was eagerly looking forward to my involvement with the carnival but I was equally very sad indeed at the thought of Grant leaving me at the end of the day. Grant and I had not only 'gelled' but we had also become very close friends. He is a man of great integrity and he had been an extremely efficient 'minder' during our period together.

It was decided that first I would push halfway to Worcester. Grant would then drive me back to take part in the Kidderminster carnival before finally returning me to the spot where I would complete the other half of my push to Worcester Fire Station.

A rendezvous had already been arranged from where we would be escorted to our day's final destination. On this Saturday, 17th June, the sun was already shining brightly which promised a gorgeous day for the carnival. I started my push early, as I wanted to complete as much mileage as I could before returning to Kidderminster. The more ground I covered during the first half of my push, the less I would have to complete later.

One of the Kidderminster firefighters, Chuck, walked at my side, optimistically carrying a red plastic bucket in anticipation. The first half went well and people gave generously as we went by. I then returned to town where I had the honour of leading the long procession, which included Brass Bands, Morris dancers, enthusiastic and very smartly uniformed little Majorettes and cheerleaders as well as highly decorated floats. The atmosphere was fantastic. The procession was relentlessly cheered and waved on by crowds of people before eventually ending in the grounds of the town's spacious park. Here there were numerous sideshows, candyfloss stalls and a travelling fair. I met children in wheelchairs, tramps, numerous dignitaries and I was again interviewed and photographed by the press. I also met lots of police officers who gave generously to my fund and we had numerous pictures taken together. Although, again, there were collectors for local charities, this did not prevent me from receiving a lot of money for *my* fund. It was a case of 'dog eat dog' and I had no qualms about collecting as much money as I could while the opportunity was there! Finally, it was time for me to press on. I still had a few more miles to go before I would be able to settle down to a nice hot dinner and a warm bed for the night.

Grant duly deposited me back at just over the halfway mark to resume my push. Surprisingly, even though it was a very hot day and I was sweating profusely, I felt full of energy and it didn't seem

Mayoral greeting, Kidderminster

long before I was tucked in behind my two-machine escort on to Worcester.

When we reached the town, our entourage clogged the streets and brought the whole town to a standstill. Here again, the cash flowed from generous donors. Finally, we made it. I was welcomed at the very big and very old fire station. However, the building's size was extremely deceiving. Once inside the establishment, the yard was very small indeed and space was at a premium. Inside the station, things were different and facilities were not compromised in any way. The old building housed a substantial kitchen, spacious canteen and a big dormitory.

In no time 'Big Dave', the Benevolent Fund rep, who was the Leading Firefighter of the watch, (and who was also on kitchen duty) immediately placed the usual mug of hot tea on the table before us. As Grant vanished back to the van to retrieve his bits and bobs to accompany him on his long journey home I remained chatting to Dave, informing him of our many 'adventures'. Grant returned a short time later and this time he was accompanied by Art, who had just arrived, leaving the hire car outside for Grant to drive back up to Dundee. The three of us then joined the night watch for their evening meal. After dinner, Grant eventually rose from the table and, shaking my hand, he wished me the best of luck for the rest of my push. After saying our mutual goodbyes, Grant finally made his exit. Art accompanied him down to his vehicle before returning to join me in the canteen.

I brought Art fully up to date with events so far (as no doubt had Grant) then our host, Big Dave, took the pair of us up to the dormitory and allocated us each a bed. I spent the rest of the evening watching television while Art went off for a pint. Eventually I went up to my bed, updated my diary and after putting my mobile phone on charge, climbed into bed and slid beneath the sheets. Another day over and another day nearer (the so far elusive) Land's End!

Chapter Twenty
Benevolence from a Boot Sale,
Tipple from a Tavern

Day Thirty-one

AFTER THE CREWS returned from their second shout of the night at
7.00 a.m. I rose from my bed. This time, I found that I was not first
up. Art had beaten me to it. After the ritual of my wash and brush up
I joined everyone in the canteen for tea and toast. The sun was again
shining brightly and it looked like being another hot day.

Art prepared the van for the day's trek as shifts changed at 9.00
a.m. Eventually, after everyone had completed their early morning
chores we all sat down to a hearty full English breakfast. Once we
were all fully fed, 'booted and spurred', Art and I were taken up to
the station's Brigade control room and introduced to the female
staff. The ladies showed us the Brigade's sophisticated, top of the
range communications equipment and gave us a very impressive
demonstration as to how the emergency services were dispatched to
cope with various incidents and scenarios. Art and I then went next
door to meet the police. They also showed us around their
headquarters and control room. I found our little tours very
interesting, as no doubt did Art. Having served operationally in *both*
services I enjoyed the unique privilege of being able to 'talk shop' to
my ex-colleagues at each venue.

Our day's trek started with Art taking numerous photographs of
old buildings of historical interest as we ventured out through the
town. Some of these fine old buildings dated from as far back as the
year 1400. We were escorted by a big American 4x4 E.T. (emergency

tender) with a crew of two, Dick and Phil. Dick drove while Phil walked alongside me carrying the usual bucket, as well as a portable radio in his shirt pocket. There was not a cloud in the beautiful blue sky and temperatures quickly soared.

As we negotiated a long steep climb out of the town centre towards the 'sticks', we passed a church with a very high steeple known as 'Glover's Needle'. Never one to miss such an opportunity, Art duly photographed the impressive looking building as we passed.

Once out into the country we made steady progress in the searing heat. We were regularly handed donations from motorists as our progress was being continually announced via local radio. Dick, sitting high up in the 4x4, spotted from his vantage point, activity in a field far ahead and I heard him inform Phil via the radio. I became very frustrated because, due to the high grass verges and hedges, I couldn't see what was going on from my lowly position nearer the ground. Phil eventually discovered that a large car boot sale was being held in an equally large field. Phil announced his 'find' to Dick via his radio. I heard Dick's crackling response suggesting we visit the site and wander around with our bucket. What a *great* idea!

Car boot sale stall holder donates

Our little procession turned into the field and we moved along the lanes of vehicles and vans. We received lots of cash from the 'stall holders' and their customers, then we stopped for a cold drink and an ice cream from the ever-present ice cream vendor.

The temperature now, at mid-day, was in the 90s! Having finally exhausted our unexpected cash supply from the Boot Sale, we ventured back, out onto the open road. Half an hour later we were about to pass a large hotel on the opposite side of the road. There were a lot of people sitting outside at tables quaffing copious amounts of ice-cold drinks. Already my mouth was watering as I had one *hell* of a thirst. I looked across enviously and saw that some of the people were waving and gesticulating to us. They were shouting and calling us over. Dick had obviously spotted what was going on as well. He pulled onto the grass verge and parked his vehicle, closely followed by Art. We all went over to the pub and were instantly inundated with ice-cold, refreshing drinks from numerous patrons, embarrassingly hailing us as *heroes*.

A young lady went to Phil and handed him a £5 note. Her male friend appeared with a tray full of drinks and four packets of crisps. Such generosity made me realise just *how* wonderful some people really are. They told us that they were aware of our 'end-to-end' endeavour having either seen us on TV or read about us in the press. This again, greatly enhanced the contents and weight of our bucket considerably.

We finished our most welcome drinks and thanked everyone for their kindness and moved on yet again. I had the discomfort of having more long, steep hills to climb. The intense heat made my efforts more strenuous. I was sweating buckets and my clothes were thoroughly soaked.

Eventually our escort had to leave us and return home to Worcester. Art and I thanked the two profusely and once again I was sad to lose such great company. I pushed on and on, up the numerous hills until we were again met by a Brigade Land Rover from the retained fire station at Tewkesbury. Our new escort, Dean, was another who had given us his *own time* to ensure our safe passage to his beautiful, picturesque town on the banks of the equally beautiful river Severn.

Even before I actually entered Tewkesbury, people who were out walking, on seeing the little convoy led by a wheelchair, knew instantly who we were. Pedestrians crossed the road to hand me donations. One lady took me by surprise as, after dropping a few coins into my bucket, she then, not only asked could she take my picture, but also asked me for my *autograph*! I signed the piece of card she offered, feeling as though I'd been elevated to the status of a pop star!

We eventually arrived at the little fire station on the edge of town. To my utter surprise, as Art and I entered the station, we were given a tumultuous welcome by the firefighters and their families.

Similarly, as with our previous benevolent Scottish welcome up at far away Slamannan, there was a table bearing a large amount of food and a big pot of tea. I was certainly ready to eat and even though I must have smelled a bit 'iffy' due to my day's long and sweaty push, I ravishingly attacked the sandwiches on the table before me.

Knowing we wanted to freshen up and sort our things out, the throng kindly left us after half an hour or so. A few arranged to meet us later at one of the local pubs. It would be another night on the floor for us and Art busied himself with bringing our sleeping bags and cases into the station while I went to wash and change.

Later, much cleaner and fresher and no doubt smelling a lot sweeter, I joined Art and we made our way to our evening's rendezvous, a popular and quaint old pub on the riverbank called The Black Bear. We sat outside on the patio of this extremely popular watering hole and savoured the beautiful views of the river Severn. As we watched the swans aimlessly drifting up and down on the calm, slow moving river we were joined by Dave, one of the firefighters and his wife Cheryl. The couple brought their daughter Kayleigh and her eight-year-old wheelchair bound brother Christopher along to meet Art and I. Young Christopher suffered from multiple schlerosis and was keen to demonstrate his own (many and varied) wheelchair skills to me. A number of courageous ducks came ashore after negotiating the steep riverbank. They waddled about amongst the tables to the delight of the patrons, audaciously seeking a share from those who were consuming a meal or snack.

After spending a couple of very pleasant hours enjoying the warm, balmy evening with our fire hosts, Art and I finally made our way back to our comfortable 'floor' for the night.

Before enveloping ourselves snugly into our sleeping bags, Art made a final brew of tea which we consumed with relish and I rang Chris and my daughter Jo to let them know that all was well.

We had now completed almost three-quarters of our long, mammoth haul. Slowly, but surely, we were getting there!

Chapter Twenty One
Bare Boobs and Soda

Day Thirty-two

AFTER A REFRESHING, good night's, *undisturbed* slumbers (the jinx must have had a night off) Art and I treated ourselves to a rare 'lie in' and didn't get up until 8.00 a.m.

As I opened the curtains, bright sunshine entered the room to tell us we were going to enjoy another warm and pleasant summer's day.

Due to the day's push being a *mere* 15 miles we decided to set off at 10.00 a.m. as, by then, the town would *hopefully* be busy with crowds of shoppers and tourists. As we set off, the station's machine and also the Station Commander, Peter Lines kindly escorted us. We had the added privilege of the Commander's wife riding along with us on her bicycle. We proceeded through town and received a large amount of cash from generous donors who congratulated us on our endeavours. The crew mingled with the crowds on both sides of the narrow road through town. We stopped at a local café and the proprietor kindly furnished Art and I with bacon sandwiches and mugs of tea.

The push to Gloucester was pleasant but very hot. Our fire escort only stayed with us as far as the end of the Tewkesbury High Street as the crew, being retained, had to resume their own *full time* employment. Once again we had to part company with a brilliant bunch of men who nevertheless ensured that we were left with very happy and valued memories.

During the push, Art ensured that I was continually and adequately supplied with liquids due to the searing heat. As I trundled along approaching the outskirts of Gloucester, I saw an attractive, blonde-haired young lady striding along ahead of me. Eventually I caught up with her and asked her how far I had to go before reaching the town's fire station. The friendly lady informed me that there were still a couple of miles to go, but as she passed the fire station on her way home she would walk with me to show the way.

I accepted her offer with gratitude. The voluptuous lady wore a very short skirt, displaying vast amounts of thigh and a flimsy top, which also emphasised her (very ample) charms. We chatted and, as we wandered along together I received a call on my mobile. It was Art. He had been 'monitoring proceedings' as he observed me from his vantage point three hundred yards behind. 'I know *exactly* what you're little game is Swasie and I'm going to tell Matron!' he bantered, referring to Chris, my mentor back home.

We continued on and I saw that my female companion displayed a tattoo at the top of her arm. After having travelled some distance further, we were about to pass a large pub when my lady friend informed me that she fancied a cold drink. I accompanied her across the pub car park, with Art in tow. We found the premises to be closed. Not to be outdone, my blonde pal knocked on a window. The landlord then opened the window and informed us that he had closed early due to lack of custom. However, after being informed of our trek and our 'dire need' of a drink, he unhesitatingly supplied Art and I with a cold pint of iced blackcurrant and soda and 'Blondie' with a pint of chilled lager. As we lounged against the wall enjoying our refreshing, cold drinks in the sunshine 'Blondie' asked me what I did for a living. Noticing her tattoo I *jokingly* told her I had been a 'Professional tattoo '*inspector*'! She seemed puzzled and asked me to elaborate. Realising she was actually taking me seriously, I informed her that I checked peoples' tattoos to ensure they were clean and free from infection. I asked the lady if she had any other tattoos. She informed me that she had one on her left shoulder. I asked if I could check if it was 'okay' and she turned and pulled her top aside to reveal the multi-coloured artistic example of body abuse. 'Yes, that's okay'

I confirmed and asked her, 'Any more?' The lady hesitated and with a slight blush, informed me that she had one on her breast. 'Let's have a look' I asked, adding, 'You've got to be ultra careful having tattoos put there'. The lady hesitatingly repeated, 'It's – it's on my – breast'. I hastily informed her, hoping I sounded professionally clinical, 'Oh don't be embarrassed, the *least* thing I'm interested in is the sight of a female breast'. I went on to emphasise, 'It's the *tattoo* I'm concerned about so let's have a look to make sure it's been done properly and check that there's no sign of infection'. Art looked on bemused. Neither of us, in our wildest *dreams*, had expected my 'tattoo inspector' dribble to be taken seriously.

However, to the utter amazement of Art and I, 'Blondie' said, 'Well I suppose it's best to be sure' and promptly opened her top, lifted her bra and exposed her large breasts to reveal a small tattoo near her left nipple. I had extreme difficulty stifling my giggles as I scrutinised the 'beautiful' little picture before me and, trying to look deadly serious, I finally looked up and said authoritatively, 'Mmmm, yes that's okay'! I couldn't *believe* my adlibbing banter furnished such a result. That was *definitely* one for the 'mammary' bank!

Our eventual arrival at the main fire station at Gloucester revealed that we had a large 'reception committee' waiting for us. The press was also in attendance to greet our arrival. Photographs were taken as Art and I were introduced to the crews as they stood alongside their machines in the sunshine. Our happy gathering was surprisingly enhanced further when two members of the Merseyside Fire Brigade control room staff, Anne, Jack and Lynette Blackburne visited us. Later, the two ladies, Art and I enjoyed a fine meal at the Four Mile House Restaurant near Brookethorpe.

Finally, the evening came to a close and the two ladies left us to continue their holiday travels whilst Art and I made our way back to Gloucester Fire Station. After Art had counted and bagged yet another large amount of cash we had a cup of tea with the lads at supper time then made for our comfortable beds for the night, wondering if the 'Jinx' would be with us again this time.

Day Thirty-three

After the traditional full English breakfast Art and I set off, escorted by a machine escort for the first two miles. On reaching the car park of a superstore we all came to a halt outside the large Tesco store. The store's Manageress, a very kind lady named Bal, arranged for two of her staff to furnish us all with cold drinks. Bal also kindly donated a generous amount of cash to our bucket, as did many of her patrons. The fire engine drew a large number of children who were allowed access to the machine. Their parents donated generously to our fund as their offsprings sat behind the large steering wheel 'dashing off to imaginary fires'!

Art and I then moved on alone as our escort returned to the station. The sky darkened and once again the rain came to ensure I received another soaking! Some miles further along our route, a television crew from Central TV filmed my progress as I pushed up a long, steep hill in the rain. Shortly after their departure the rain conveniently stopped as I was then intercepted by Gloucester FM Radio and interviewed live on air.

The remainder of the day's 21-mile, 7-hour push was uneventful and I finally reached the little village of Wotton-under Edge where my day's endeavours were concluded. A young retained firefighter, Ben, met Art and I at the fire station. Shortly after, Chris the Station Officer arrived and showed us the floor on which we would be sleeping that night.

Young Ben's girlfriend worked at the Swan Hotel in the village and she arranged for Art and I to savour the gastronomic delights of her establishment. After Art had counted the contents of my bucket, we enjoyed a large meal of T-bone steak and chips, courtesy of the Swan Hotel. After our meal Art stayed on to enjoy a couple of pints, however, I left to get back and into my sleeping bag for a much-wanted sleep.

Day Thirty-four

After a night's restless and periodic slumbers, due to the sound of howling winds and storms, I reluctantly rose to join Art for a hot mug of tea at 7.00 a.m. Although by this time the weather had calmed down a bit, it was still raining. I *really* looked forward to another day's soaking! By the time we set off at 9.45 a.m. the rain had stopped. However, I now had to fight a strong head wind, which made the going *very* tough, especially on the long hills.

Eventually, an appliance from Bristol met me and again the crew accompanied me all the way to their base. As we travelled through the large City of Bristol, the Sub Officer announced our arrival and the purpose of the push to all and sundry via the machine's PA system. His initiative and informative rhetoric brought an instant response from shoppers and motorists. The booming announcements even caused the town's winos and dropouts to stagger out into the roadway and top up my bucket. I shall always remember their (inebriated) generosity.

On arrival at the station, I dined with the Brigade's 'Top Brass' after which we all left for a press photo-shoot with the famous Clifton Suspension Bridge behind us as a back drop. We were graced with the presence of His Worship the Lord Mayor of Bristol who presented me with a shield as well as donating generously to my bucket. Thankfully the weather was kind and allowed our activities to be completed unhindered. I had the pleasure of meeting a number of foreign tourists who honoured me by asking to have their pictures taken with me! After being interviewed by HTV newsreader Peter Power, Art and I returned to Bristol Fire Station with our hosts, Sub Officer Windows, Lenny Angus and Dick Green. I was afforded the privilege of having the Station Officer's room for the night. After dinner I phoned home, completed my diary then made for the warm confines of my bed.

I had now completed 700 miles.

Chapter Twenty Two
Pedal Power and More 'Exposures'

Day Thirty-five

EARLY RISE THIS morning! I was surprised to see the cleaning lady already at work after my morning wash and brush-up at 6.00 a.m. The weather again decided to be naughty. High winds and rain, just great! I could look forward to another exciting, soaking and weather-beaten day.

I started my day's push to Weston-super-Mare accompanied by a keen jogger, firefighter Malcolm Hordan. Mal decided to walk with me for a 'few' miles with a collecting bucket after finishing his night's duty. Unfortunately our morning's dual efforts were to no avail and our buckets remained empty. Due to the heavy rain and high winds, there were no donors courageous enough to brave the elements. Mal left me after three miles to jog his soggy way back to Bristol. His kind effort *and his company*, in his own time, were *very* much appreciated.

I continued my sodden battle against the elements until a machine and crew (Blue Watch) eventually met me from the well known resort of Weston-super-Mare. We made our way down a long hill and I saw a little store almost secreted among the trees at the side of the road. I signalled our entourage to pull in while I (cheekily) introduced myself to the shop's proprietor and explained our presence. To my surprise, the proprietor's wife informed me that she used to live in Wirral and had known my wife Marje very well. We received a *more* than generous donation from the kind couple as well as a cold drink before we resumed our journey. The weather improved and the rain gave way to become warm and dry.

Our buckets started to fill as we made our way along into the outskirts of the well known holiday town of Weston-super-Mare. Our route to the fire station took us along the Weston-super-Mare seafront and through the friendly town. When we finally arrived, I was still soaking wet from the earlier downpours. I was extremely uncomfortable and the first thing was to wash and get myself into warm and dry clothes. After achieving this number one priority, I joined Art and my new hosts in the large canteen. Once I had a mug of hot tea in my hands all was okay again and the world was my oyster!

After a fantastic dinner of chicken Kiev, new potatoes and salad followed by strawberries and clotted cream, Art and I accompanied a crew along the seafront optimistically rattling our buckets.

As we made our way along, a similar scenario reminiscent to that of our Stirling 'adventure' manifested itself. Numerous female holidaymakers and night-time revellers in various states of dress and inebriation stood cheering the fire engine as it passed them by. Many of the ladies flashed their naked boobs at the crew. Amazingly, I can categorically state that this is *not* an uncommon occurrence! I have truly, *personally* witnessed such behaviour being directed at uniformed fire personnel on *many* occasions. This type of scenario was totally unknown when I was a member of the service but now however, in this day and age, it is indicative as to how times (and morals) have changed!

Our 'nocturnal' fundraising venture, like Stirling, generated a *lot* of cash to our charity – as well as enhancing the morale of the Weston-super-Mare Fire Brigade! By the time we had returned to the station and put the machine away, it was time for 'supper'. The wind and rain returned just as we entered the warm and protective confines of the station.

After settling down for the night, I lay beneath the warm sheets and the sound of the wind howling and the rain battering against the windows soon sent me to sleep.

Day Thirty-six

AT 7.15 A.M. I rose to complete my ablutions and ready myself for the day's push. I then made my way downstairs (on my bottom) with my chair and ventured along to the canteen. I joined Art, who was busy completing his log and other, equally important 'end-to-end' documentation. The lads of the night watch, who would be going off duty at 9.00 a.m., soon furnished me with a mug of hot, sweet tea and a couple of slices of buttered toast. Thankfully, the rain now appeared to have stopped and, although there were occasional outbreaks of sunshine, the wind insisted on blowing hard to ensure I would have to endure a very hard day.

At 9.00 a.m. members of the day watch paraded for duty allowing their night duty colleagues to go home to a day's 'hibernation'. After parade, the new oncoming watch checked their machines and numerous sophisticated items of equipment, before treating me to a *most* amusing spectacle.

A photo-shoot had been arranged and I pushed outside expecting one of the machines to be driven out onto the station forecourt. A machine *was* already outside in position on the station forecourt however, its crew had so far failed to put in an appearance. I sat in my chair wondering where the lads were, when suddenly out of the station came a red, four-wheeled cycle being *pedalled* by firefighters. The 'machine' had a blue light, a bell and a ladder! I was totally fascinated and amused at the sight of such an unusual spectacle. The 'machine' was conceived *and* manufactured entirely by the men and women of Weston-super-Mare Fire Brigade for charity fundraising purposes and visits to local schools. This is typical of the innovative creativity and pure ingenuity of Brigade members throughout the whole of the service in their continual quests to raise money for charitable causes.

Finally we left our seaside 'home' to head south and resume our long trek to, a still far away, Land's End. Today's push would take me to Bridgwater, 23 miles away. Although the weather was mild, I was

Weston-super-Mare charity 'vehicle'

however, confronted by a continual, strong head wind. On leaving the station with Art and my fire engine escort we again went along the seafront and entered the town. The crew dismounted and walked through the town with me, collecting on each side of the narrow streets. Suddenly, they were summoned to mount their machine. They had received 'a shout'! One minute I was with the lads, the next, they had completely 'evaporated' and I was left totally alone in a crowded, unfamiliar resort and completely ignorant as to where I should make for next. The machine drove off and of Art there was no sign. I made my way back to the seafront and turned left. *Thankfully*, I had made the right decision which was confirmed when I pushed along the promenade and saw a sign pointing towards my goal, Bridgwater.

A short time later I breathed a sigh of relief when I saw the familiar sight of our white van in my mirror as it flashed its headlights to make me aware of its presence. Thankfully, Art had found me and was with me once again! As I approached the end of the lengthy road along the seafront my fire engine escort returned to join me from their (false alarm) call. The lads stayed with Art and I for two miles then returned to base leaving the two of us to trundle on alone along the busy A38. Eventually I saw the welcome and reassuring sight of a fire engine approaching me from the opposite direction. The machine flashed its lights and sounded its 'two tone' klaxon horns as it passed. It then turned round and pulled in front of me to lead the way. It was in fact the new Green Watch escort from our next port of call, Bridgwater.

As always, the considerate crew accompanied me on foot and collected enthusiastically. We reached Bridgwater and continued to enhance the contents of our buckets as we passed through the town to the fire station. We were greeted on arrival by the Brigade Benevolent Fund rep, Kevin Mitchum.

Art and I were ushered into the big building and shown to our 'sleeping quarters'. After placing our belongings on our bunks, we returned to the canteen for a well-earned brew of tea. During our introductory cuppa to the rest of the station crews, Kevin presented me with a Shield bearing the Somerset Fire Brigade coat of arms together with a shirt bearing the Brigade badge.

A short time later we had two surprise visitors. An elderly couple, who lived on the outskirts of Bridgwater but originally came from Liverpool, heard of our visit via the press and media. Old Harry, an ex-Liverpool bobby, and his charming wife Minnie, both in their eighties decided to pay us a visit at the station. Unknown to me, Harry possessed two of my books, *Off the Cuff* and *If the Cap Fits*. He proudly showed them to me and asked me to sign them. I endorsed each with a warm message 'to a 'fellow copper' of long, long ago'.

Harry was delighted. I felt very humbled at his request and I deemed this, and their visit, to be a very great honour. The two eventually left and later, after Art and I enjoyed a roast dinner with the night shift, Art ventured out into the night to seek a couple of pints from the local hostelries. I retired to my bed and 'crashed out' for the night.

Day Thirty-seven

During the night the crews were turned out twice. Eventually peace and tranquillity returned and they were able to snatch a couple of hours sleep after returning from their second 'shout' at 4.00 a.m. Everyone, including Art and I, rose from our beds at 6.45 a.m.

After breakfast (and the usual photo shoot for posterity) we were escorted out of Bridgwater, by the same day shift (Blue Watch) crew, who had escorted us *into* town yesterday. My escort and I again received numerous kind donations from the people of the town as we made our way along. On the edge of town I again had the pleasure of meeting old Harry and Minnie. The two had been waiting patiently for us to pass their house and Harry presented me with a little plastic 'Fireman Sam' (which I treasure to this day) and Minnie gave me a bag of sweets. What an extreme honour it was for me to have met and befriended such a fantastically wonderful couple. After leaving the couple and continuing on, it was soon time for my escort to leave me. They bade Art and I a fond farewell before returning to their station. Although the weather was warm and dry, the winds were still strong and blustery. My 'target for today' was Wellington Fire Station at Taunton.

After a few miles pushing and receiving a number of donations from kind motorists and local residents, my machine escort from Taunton met me. Another surprise came about as we pushed along. A vehicle stopped and a lady and gentleman alighted and came over to me. 'Hi Swasie, I couldn't believe my eyes when I saw you on the road! How are you?' the lady asked. The lady called Tina, now living in Taunton, used to live next door to Marje and I back home in West Kirby, Wirral and was once my son's friend and schoolmate. She introduced her husband to me and we chatted for a while. Needless to say, I received a generous donation from Tina and her equally generous husband.

We moved on and finally reached Taunton. We made our way through to the town centre where we stopped to meet the people of the delightful town while the crew stood with their collection buckets. We all enjoyed the warm sun as the wind had finally dropped to a slight breeze. A young lady in a wheelchair pushed herself over to me. 'Hi, my name's Sally', she said. She told us that she was waiting for her father to arrive to accompany her around the town shopping. Sally informed me that she had read about my fundraising endeavours in various papers and disability magazines.

I gave her a signed copy of *Wheelchair Pilot* as we sat chatting. Her father then arrived to meet her and, after introducing himself, father and daughter then left to commence their shopping spree. Whilst we were chatting to our 'bucket feeding' public we were joined by two pretty lady traffic wardens and a local constable.

After two hours 'boosting our tan' while we collected in the sunny town centre, we eventually continued on to the fire station. On our subsequent arrival after the day's lengthy push we were met by the station's commander. The senior officer kindly presented me with a shirt bearing the logo of the Brigade before presenting Art with a souvenir Brigade badge. I was introduced to Sub Officer, Phil Lovegrove who informed me about a new innovation he and his brigade were introducing. I was asked if I would write an article about the introduction of a 'Fire Cadet' scheme in my newspaper column (at the time I was the resident columnist in the national newspaper of the service, the *Fire News*). I gathered all the relevant information, requesting pictures of any cadets and promised that I would write a lengthy, illustrated article for the *Fire* News. My brigade hosts were extremely pleased with the prospect of their new scheme receiving heavy publicity.

After dinner I watched a little TV, but as I was so tired I finally placed my mobile phone on charge, completed my diary and retired for the night at 10.00 p.m. There was no sign of Art. Presumably he had gone to seek comfort and solace from 'Mrs Tipple's pint pots'!

Chapter Twenty Three
Beauty, Serenity and Tragedy

Day Thirty-eight

I ENJOYED MY stay at Wellington Fire Station. The Sub Officer of Blue Watch possessed an extremely quick wit and acute sense of humour, which appealed to me greatly. The lads loved him, however, they also knew that he was *the boss*! A young member of the Watch informed me that his parents lived quite near to me back home in Wirral. As he never stopped talking about Wirral I nicknamed him the 'Wirral Squirrel'. The name has stuck to him ever since!

What a terrific send off the lads gave us as we left Wellington Station. Both Blue and Green Watches turned out in force to wave us goodbye. The crews presented me with a cheque for £25 and others dropped cash into my bucket. I pushed off with just Art as my escort. Again, a beautiful blue and cloudless sky promised another hot day. Unfortunately, there were numerous hills along the day's entire route, which I would have to negotiate. My 25-mile push for today would take me to the quiet little town of Tiverton. Except for the occasional donation from a passing motorist, the push was mainly uneventful, apart from the incessant short, sharp hills which caused me to sweat profusely as I pushed onwards and upwards under the relentless glare of the hot, summer sun.

As I rumbled on I received phone calls from Matron and my daughter Jo. A police car passed by, flashing its blue strobe light in acknowledgement before vanishing over the top of the next hill. Eventually, as I rounded a bend at the top of a long hill, I passed the large, roadside sign bearing the message 'Welcome to Devon'. After the strain of the constant hills I had been negotiating, the sight of this sign gave me a tremendous boost. It felt absolutely fantastic to think that I had now entered the next to last county of my nearly 1,000 mile push. My morale and my sagging stamina were boosted considerably. I pushed on with tremendous zeal. It must have been purely psychological, but my day's push now seemed easy.

Art and I arrived at what appeared to be a ghost town. Tiverton seemed deserted. Perhaps they knew we were coming! Art's navigational skills successfully guided us to the town's retained fire station. The Station Officer, his Sub Officer Steve and two of the firefighters met us on arrival. After formalities were completed and we were shown to our 'sleeping quarters' (the snooker room floor!) Steve took Art and I to his nearby home. There, we were introduced to his wheelchair-bound wife Colleen. We spent an hour chatting and drinking tea before returning to the station to unpack.

Art and I later dined at the beautifully picturesque Fisherman's Cot Restaurant where we enjoyed a sumptuous mixed grill. During our meal the proprietor Mr Tim Harrison-Jones (who was also the establishment's highly professional chef) came to us and informed us that, as he was aware of our marathon push, the meal was 'on the house'. He also gave me £20 for my bucket.

The benevolent restaurateur went on to recite an extremely sad tale relating to the nearby beautiful stone bridge which spanned the river Exe that passed alongside the restaurant. I watched the same river outside as it meandered along and flowed by over rocks, enhancing the peaceful, panoramic beauty of the Devon countryside. This beautiful 'God's little acre' had not *always* been such a tranquil paradise however, as our host went on to elaborate. Years ago, he informed us, a group of scouts were camping on the riverbank near the little bridge. During the night, as the adventurous youngsters lay sleeping in their tents, torrential rain fell causing the river to rise rapidly. The calm, babbling river soon became a raging torrent and in no time it rose up and over its banks. The poor defenceless boys were swept away and many were drowned. The horrible tragedy affected everyone.

View from Bickleigh Bridge (over troubled waters)

Staying at the Fisherman's Cot at that time, were the well-known songwriters Simon and Garfunkel. The tragedy affected them both so much, the traumatised duo wrote the famous heart rending song 'Bridge Over Troubled Waters'. This story, and the song, are now *indelibly* printed in my mind and will remain so for ever.

After our much appreciated meal (and donation) we concluded our very enjoyable and informative conversation and Art and I returned home to the 'floor'! As we made our way back to the station for our night's 'hibernation', I couldn't stop thinking about those poor scouts. As I look back now, I think about how ironic things are as, some time after this push, I too was swept under the very same bridge and over the fierce weir at Bickleigh. I was to come to grief here after being thrown from my canoe whilst negotiating the 32-mile 'Exe Descent'; an endurance testing canoe trip from Tiverton to Exeter with the Royal Marines along that same, fast flowing, dangerous and unforgiving river Exe. Every one of the five canoeists were thrown from their crafts during that arduous and physically demanding trip.

Back at the station, I climbed into my sleeping bag and, with the scouts still in my thoughts, I fell asleep.

Day Thirty-nine

A beautiful ornithological 'Dawn Chorus' brought me pleasantly from my slumbers at 6.00 a.m. and again, the sky was devoid of cloud. Art and I rose to wash and pack away our sleeping bags before sitting down to tea and toast. Art checked the van's oil and water levels before completing his log and paper work. Finally we were ready to set off once again. Today was an early start as we had 28 miles to cover before we made our next port of call at far away Oakhampton. We also had to ensure we reached The Exchange Hotel on Crediton High Street before noon!

Once we ensured that all was tidy, Art and I endorsed the station memo book, acknowledging the wonderful hospitality afforded us

The Exchange Hotel, Crediton High Street

by the firefighters of Tiverton. We left the station and made our way deeper into the heart of Devon along the quiet and narrow country roads. I was undoubtedly passing through some of the most beautiful scenery the country could offer and the descriptive term 'Glorious Devon' seemed very apt. Slowly, we meandered on past the beautiful Fisherman's Cot Restaurant and crossed the little bridge. Again I couldn't help thinking of the scouts, and the song 'Bridge Over Troubled Waters' continually ran through my mind as I pushed over the little bridge. The sun rose steadily up into the blue sky and very soon I was uncomfortably hot and sweating profusely. The continual steep hills never seemed to go downwards, always upwards! I had a 'gun to my head' this morning, having to make the ten miles to Crediton's Exchange Hotel for mid-day at the *very* latest. The kind licensee and his wife were to give a generous donation to our bucket as well as hosting us for lunch.

I was met by a mobile police patrol as I was about to enter the busy little town of Crediton. The officer introduced himself as Andy and informed me that he recognised me from my column in *Police News*. Andy threw some coins into my bucket and led our little procession into the town. He took us straight to our intended oasis, The Exchange Hotel. We arrived *almost* on time and were greeted by 'mine hosts' Stephanie and Michael Drew. As promised, each gave a substantial donation to our bucket and provided us with an equally substantial meal. Andy kindly remained 'on station' outside and when we resumed our journey, he escorted us for a couple of miles out of town and on to the 'open road'.

The searing heat and constant hill climbs started to take their toll. For the first time I started to become seriously dehydrated. At one stage I thought I was going to pass out. I was forced to make frequent stops to gather breath and strength during my many climbs. Art could see I was in trouble and constantly fed me copious amounts of water. Due to the unrelenting hot sun and my continual loss of body fluid, today's push had become my worst day so far. My strength and stamina appeared to have left me.

Art pulled off the road and stopped me. He insisted that we stop for half an hour. His philosophy worked. After drinking pints and pints of water and consuming a bar of chocolate, as well as Art unceremoniously pouring a bottle of water over me, I was eventually able to continue. As I resumed I felt ten times better, I was now 'fully fit' again! We stopped for a short break as we passed down a steep hill through the village of Bow where I consumed a couple of fruit ices before carrying on.

Finally, after what seemed an eternity, I rolled my chair into the more than welcome hospitable and protective confines of Oakhampton Retained Fire Station where we were greeted warmly by Sub Officer Ian Donovan.

After sorting out our sleeping arrangements Art and I went to a nearby pub for our evening meal. I left Art at the pub enjoying a few well-deserved pints. I made straight back to the station and dived into my sleeping bag. The moment my head sank into my pillow I almost immediately fell into a deep sleep.

Day Forty

This morning, I again woke to the 'Dawn Chorus' but the tune, 'Bridge Over Troubled Waters' still haunted me. My imagination ran riot as I kept thinking of the young scouts that were swept away as they slept. Although I have witnessed, attended and had to deal with *many* gory, sad and horrific scenarios during my service, I just could not get the proprietor's rendition of the horrific tragedy out of my mind.

After yesterday's most tiresome and physically demanding efforts I looked forward to today's *short* push of 22 miles. I would ensure that, as today was undoubtedly going to be another hot one, I would keep myself 'topped up' with cold liquids. As usual, Art and I endorsed the station memo book with our profuse gratitude to our magnificent hosts, and then set off on our day's trek. We called in at the police station for a cup of tea with the officers. Everyone we met unhesitatingly gave to our bucket. We all posed for photographs outside the station before resuming my push. I had the honour of receiving a call on my mobile from none other than the Chief Constable of Devon and Cornwall Police, Sir John Evans. This was a fantastic surprise. John was my inspector at Rose Hill, Liverpool, in the mid-sixties! Later, as Sir John was being flown in his helicopter to Buckingham Palace for a meeting with Prince Charles, he flew low and briefly hovered above an adjacent field we were passing. What a courteous *and* very much appreciated gesture from my old boss!

The day again became very hot. It was very hard going in such heat. The road was extremely busy and I was ecstatic when, at long last, I pushed past the sign bearing the name 'CORNWALL' in large letters and crossed the border into the *'final'* county.

A police van drove past in the opposite direction flashing his headlights and I waved in acknowledgement. Later, the same van passed me again and vanished up and over the brow of the hill in front of me. Once over the brow I savoured the delights of a (strictly controlled 3 mph) descent for a change. I continued down the mile-long, busy dual carriageway and saw, to my utter amazement, the white police van parked ahead in a lay-by. The van's uniformed driver stood by his van waiting for me. The sight of him standing there

Swasie enters Cornwall

Pete from Launceston with lollies for Swasie

holding two ice lollies – *for me!* was absolutely unbelievable, it was as though I was seeing a mirage! 'I thought you might need these', said 'Pete' an officer from Launceston as he handed me the two ices. He invited us to follow him to Launceston Police Station for a cold drink and a snack in the Launceston Police Station's Club. We gratefully accepted his more than welcome offer. After what seemed an age, we finally negotiated the last, steep hill to the station.

Pete took us in to the Police Club Bar where we met a number of equally hot and thirsty members of the constabulary. Art and I were plied with food and drink by the extremely hospitable police officers. Each contributed to the rattling confines of my bucket. After this most unexpected and refreshing rest, I continued my push to Launceston Fire Station for a wash and brush up. I changed into clean and dry clothing, and then Art drove us to our overnight accommodation at Bodmin Fire Station. We would return in the morning to resume our push from where we left off today.

We arrived at Bodmin and I met a number of the firefighters, many of whom were to become my very close, lifelong friends. I would later push with two of these firefighters; first with ex-Para and Falklands veteran Richie Helleur across the inhospitable Falklands Islands; later with firefighter, Nigel Honey on a 286-mile push from the Whitehouse, Washington to 'Ground Zero' in New York; and later still with Nigel through the equally inhospitable 'Death Valley' in Nevada.

The crews sent out for 'takeaway' meals, then we all made for the little canteen for our dinner of curried beef and rice. Unknown to Art and I a buffet and social evening had been arranged in our honour! Chief Fire Officer Mick Howells and his senior officers, ADO Mike Perriton, ADO Brian Crowle and members of the Fire Services Benevolent Fund committee attended. The evening's social gathering was held at the station. I finally had to excuse myself from the evening's revelry and sneaked away to my sleeping bag to sleep the night away on the hose room floor Art remained until the night's 'session' was concluded!

Chapter Twenty Four
Snakes and Ladders – Cakes and Adders

Day Forty-one

OUR BODMIN ACCOMMODATION was very uncomfortable. We slept amongst a room full of hose reels and other equipment, plus, the floor was *very* hard. However, beggars can't be choosers! Our 'Jinx' was obviously still with us as the machines were turned out twice during the night.

Art and I were up and about by 7.15 a.m. After our tea and toast we drove back to resume my push from Launceston.

We were blessed with another *very* hot summer's day. Although I love the summer and fine weather, it is very hard and most uncomfortable pushing in such heat.

I was cursing the many, very steep and lengthy climbs that seemed to go on forever. I thought my push through the Scottish Highlands had been tough but the Cornish hills were a continual test of my stamina. I pushed on and on and descended a long two-mile downhill stretch. This was great, however, I learned long ago that what goes down then also goes up! Unfortunately this was to be no exception. After my lengthy descent I then had an equally lengthy climb. I grunted and sweated as I trundled on and on under the relentless sun. After pushing for over ten miles I saw a little pimple on the top of a distant hill, the Jamaica Inn. Our escorting machine and crew would be waiting there for us. I rolled down the next hill before having to climb up to meet the lads from Bodmin. I saw what I thought was a coil of rope or hosepipe lying at the side of the road. I went to pick it up and throw it onto the grass verge but as I did so, to my horror, the 'rope' moved. It was in fact an *Adder*! Needless to say, I didn't pick it up; instead, I saluted the venomous reptile and beat a hasty retreat. The climb to Jamaica Inn seemed effortless after my brief encounter with the snake!

We stopped at the Inn for refreshments and were served by Sarah, a very charming member of the hotel staff. The young lady enquired the reason for the fire engine's presence. The crew enlightened her as to our push then they took her outside and placed her behind the wheel of their machine, explaining the functions of the various rescue and firefighting facilities on board. The very impressed lady was fascinated by the machine's various dials and rescue equipment. We chatted for a while and Sarah was invited to join us all at the fire station club bar later that evening. Sarah accepted the invitation and before we left she supplied a box of cakes for us to eat on our travels. I then set off with my new escort for Bodmin, 13 miles away. The machine led the way while the crew walked with me. After three miles we stopped for a cold drink while we consumed Sarah's delicious cakes. Rob, the Sub Officer then failed his initiative test!

Swasie and escort descending into Bodmin

Thinking (mistakenly) that it would be better if he wore his fire boots instead of his leather shoes, he duly donned the thick, hot *rubber* boots.

It was a long and very hot slog before we finally dropped down the extremely steep (and long) hill into Bodmin. Rob's rubber boots had rubbed his heels raw. Before making for the fire station, we called at Bodmin Police Station. We were all made very welcome and the sergeant made us all a brew of tea. He showed us round his station and we met a couple of officers. As I passed a room I saw a young man in civilian clothes sitting at a desk on which were some papers. I greeted him with a friendly, 'Hi, everything okay?' but he did not respond. I said, '*You* don't look very happy?' He looked up and without any trace of a smile he snarled, 'You wouldn't be happy either' and pointing to the three or four papers on his desk he went on to inform me, 'You've no idea how busy it is being in the CID'. Having spent eight years in the CID I quickly responded, 'Young man, I've been longer on a bloody *message* than you've been in the *police*, never mind the CID'. I left the disgruntled and without doubt inexperienced young pup and resumed my 'tour' of the station, much to the amusement of those that witnessed my stinging rebuke.

After leaving the police station we wandered on through the town collecting many donations from the kindly people of Bodmin. Eventually, after exchanging light-hearted banter between the crew and various shops who gave freely to our cause, we finally arrived back at Bodmin Fire Station where Art and I would be staying for a second night. We enjoyed another 'takeaway' meal of curry and rice and later, true to her word, Sarah, the lady from the Jamaica Inn, joined us all at the bar. That evening I also received a telephone call from Sir John Evans's Staff Officer Andrew Brickley wishing me well on behalf of his Chief Constable.

At the conclusion of the evening's little social gathering, I duly made for my 'sleeping quarters'; the hose room. I climbed into my warm sleeping bag and settled down on the unforgiving floor with a reel of fire hose as my pillow.

Day Forty-two

I must have slept well as I didn't hear Art come in from the bar, nor did I hear the morning's busy activities as the crews checked their machines. I was woken by the Sub Officer, Rob (of the sore feet) who informed me that breakfast was ready. After a quick wash I sat with the crew and enjoyed a full English breakfast. After we had eaten, we all paraded outside into the yard for a photo-shoot.

As we all stood and sat in position with a station machine in the background, the control room ladies joined us to enhance the pictures. Finally, all was ready. The photographer 'manned' his tripod and made final adjustments to his camera and was about to take the first of his images when suddenly, one of the firefighters, Richie Helleur, drove across the yard sounding his horn as he went off duty. He drove straight through our little gathering and scattered all and sundry in every direction. Ritchie waved as he left the yard, laughing like a drain. Not everyone saw the funny side of his jape! However, I thought it was hilarious.

After a number of successful photographs were taken, I started my long push to distant Cambourne. The Cornwall Brigade were (as was the typical 'norm') absolutely fantastic. Their kindness and warm hospitality was just great!

I was escorted by a machine and as usual its 'pedestrian' crew. Once out of town the donations still continued from motorists unabated. Two audacious firefighters even boarded a double decker bus. One collected from passengers downstairs while his colleague did likewise on the top deck. After their successful sortie they got off at a bus stop further along the road! How's that for initiative? A machine from Newquay eventually met us and also an off duty ADO, Mike Perriton joined our little procession and meandered alongside me on his mountain bike.

We were making our way up a long hill when a car pulled in front of us and stopped. Out stepped the lovely Sarah from the Jamaica Inn with a couple of boxes of cakes. We were all pleased to see her and we stopped to chat and eat her scrumptious cakes. After topping up our stamina and strength via Sarah's sustaining cuisine, we resumed our journey and bade the benevolent 'Lady Sarah' goodbye.

Further along our hot and sweaty route I received a call on my mobile. It was Radio Cornwall who proceeded to conduct a live interview on air. I mentioned Sarah and the Jamaica Inn as well as profusely thanking the population of Cornwall for their extremely kind benevolence and warm hospitality. We wandered on and on, the long hill climbs were again taking their toll on my stamina. I was losing lots of body fluid due to the relentless beating down of the hot sun. My sagging energy was however 'repaired' by the constant and incessant banter from the 'troops'. After reaching the top of a long hill I saw another similar hill had to be negotiated further on. I scolded Mike Perriton by saying abruptly, 'I thought you said that was the last hill'. Mike responded dryly, 'That *was* the last hill', but pointing ahead he continued 'and *that* one's the next!' The non-stop banter and chastisement worked wonders. 'C'mon for gawd sake, 'urry up Swasie, we 'aven't got all day' was typical of their vitriolic renderings. During our day's push I lost track of how many different machines had joined and left us.

As we passed a nursing home I was touched at the sight of the elderly patients who gathered at the windows waving to us enthusiastically. We waved back with equal vigour. Suddenly the home's Matron came out to intercept us. She asked us if we would oblige the elderly patients who not only wanted to meet us after seeing us on television, but would also like to have their picture taken with us. To a man, we were all *more* than happy to oblige. We stopped and went into the establishment to meet our 'fans'. We chatted at length with the elderly people who were so grateful for what I considered to be an extremely *small* obliging gesture by ourselves.

Matron went on to inform us that she was at first extremely apprehensive and very reluctant to ask such a favour of us. She explained at length that her reluctance was due to her having previously asked another 'end-to-end' fundraiser, a well-known sports 'celebrity' who she named, if he would oblige the old folk by allowing himself to be photographed with them. The kindly Matron told us of her very embarrassing humiliation and utter amazement on being told by the 'celebrity' to 'F--- Off'! This was *not* the first time Art and I had heard this. We had been told previously during our travels that the *same,* named man had made similar offensive and abusive comments to a group of children who, after their lengthy wait for him to arrive in their area had sought his autograph during his walk. Similar, offensive and obnoxious behaviour by the same man, was related to us by a *police officer!* He had been subjected to a torrent of abuse when he had instructed the obnoxious man and his entourage to ease traffic congestion by going one way but he abusively insisted on going another. The officer told us that the arrogant 'Mr Big' would have been arrested had it not been for the pacifying intervention of his senior officers to prevent what would have been an extremely embarrassing public 'incident'!

After spending some very enjoyable time with our aged 'fans', during which numerous pictures were taken and many donations were generously given by the staff and residents, we sadly bade them all goodbye.

We continued on but lost our escort a short time later when it was suddenly summoned away to attend an emergency. Finally we made to our destination and duly arrived at Camborne Fire Station. After a quick dash to wash and change out of my sweat-soaked and smelly clothes I joined Art to meet our kind, caring hosts. Today I had been in the saddle for *nine hours!* After a delightful meal of chips, egg and beans I couldn't resist the temptation to take to my bed for a good night's restful sleep. I excused myself and made my exit, leaving Art with the gang as I made for my bed to crash out.

Day Forty-three

After a comfortable night's slumbers I woke at 6.45 a.m. *Everyone* was already up and about, including Art. I washed and made my way to the station's 'centre of activity', the canteen. After breakfast, with my ever faithful Art tucked in behind me, I pushed along to Cambourne Police Station, astern of my fire engine escort to meet the 'cloth'. They too were absolutely great. We met the officers and staff who promptly and selflessly held a collection before presenting us with the princely sum of £57.30. As usual, a number of pictures were taken by Art, (and the police) to record our visit. The proverbial mug of tea appeared and was dutifully consumed before we were 'collected' by our fire engine escort to resume our trek.

We made our way along the busy A30 before making a detour through the pretty little village of Hayle. I was summoned into two pubs (followed by the others) and handed donations. The second pub also handed Art and I a drink of lemonade and a Cornish pasty. On the road again, I was hailed and greeted by a hooded and scrimmed SAS patrol as they drove past in their 'pink panther'. Our little trek through Hayle was well worthwhile as we netted just over £126!

Further on we again diverted and stopped for more photographs to be taken on the seafront with the picturesque St Michael's Mount in the background. As an additional bonus, a pod of dolphins duly obliged by leaping out of the water 60 yards offshore. What a beautiful neck of the woods this was.

A Green Watch crew from Penzance arrived and met us with their machine. We continued on and finally threaded our way, collecting as we went, through the winding streets and very steep little hills of Penzance. The town was crowded with tourists and holidaymakers. I had earlier passed the Helipad and watched the helicopters taking off and landing, to and from the Scilly Isles. When we finally arrived at the fire station, I was intrigued at the sight of a firefighter 'sculptured' out of a privet hedge that greeted us. Art couldn't resist committing the leafy little 'Firefighter of Foliage' to film.

Later the same evening Art and I were 'wined and dined' at a nearby Hotel, courtesy of Tim Cox from Lomax. Once our social evening drew to a close, Art and I returned for our last overnight stay on a fire station.

Our 'supper' consisted of the most gigantic Cornish pasty I have *ever* seen and this was even *accompanied by chips and peas!* The particular firefighter, who was (inevitably nearly always) the cook of the watch, had personally made each of these gigantic pasties himself. I thought the pasty was meant to be dissected to enable each man to have a piece…I was wrong! There was one similar manhole sized pasty for each member of the watch! I had a bite then decided to save the rest. I made my way to my bed and once tucked up I found that I could not get to sleep due the excitement at what I was about to achieve, which *many* thought would be impossible.

Chapter Twenty Five
The End of the 'End-to-End'

Day Forty-four — The last day

UP AT 7.00 A.M. and, after a quick wash and brush up, Art and I packed the van before enjoying a big breakfast courtesy of the 'gang' of White Watch. Art was as excited as I was. Neither of us could conceal the immense pride at what we were about to achieve today.

The crews quickly finished their chores and stayed on after the day shift parade so that photographs could be taken by the press, the Brigade photographer and Art. When the excitement eventually died down, Art, my fire engine escort and I then made off to Penzance Police Station. There I met WPC Helen Cox who gave a generous donation and she too was photographed before our final departure for Land's End, our ultimate goal.

There was still no respite in the steep hills that continually abounded. However, such was my excitement and adrenaline flow, my strength and stamina could *more* than cope. It wasn't long before we were passed by lots of people who were making their way ahead to form a welcoming party. Representatives from Duracell, one of my sponsors, were first to pass. Coaches slowly negotiated the narrow road as they passed my convoy of police and fire escorts. Everyone waved from the coaches' windows as they passed, some threw coins and a couple of bank notes fluttered down into the roadway.

My accompanying crews hastily retrieved their welcome donations from the roadway and fed them into our buckets.

Approaching Land's End

Eventually we were passed by two vintage fire engines, one of which was a turntable ladder and the other a wheeled pump escape. The crews of both machines were clad in the uniforms of their day to ensure authenticity. As the machines passed they sounded their brass bells in unison. The sight and sound brought a lump to my throat. I was then joined by ADO Mike Perriton from Bodmin. He duly gave me an almighty hug and pursed his lips as he mockingly gave me a congratulatory 'kiss', which was instantly photographed by all that were in possession of a camera! To add icing to the cake, my 'minder' Chris 'Matron' then joined our party from home. She had brought my son Ron and his partner Pam the three hundred miles so that they would be there to welcome me on arrival at the end of my lengthy push. The weather was bright, sunny and warm, which helped to create a fantastic atmosphere.

Eventually when Land's End was almost in sight we were stopped by a police officer who informed us that we were 'too early' and requested that we stop for half an hour. We all duly entered a nearby pub called 'The First and Last'. The licensee joined in the celebrations and we received numerous donations. His little pub was filled to brimming with locals, tourists and well-wishers. I was warmly greeted and congratulated by a local endurance wheelchair athlete, Billy Thornton, who kindly presented me with a large bottle of champagne.

A signal was received for us to carry on and we resumed our trek. Even from over half a mile away, I could hear the razzmatazz; bells, horns, hooters, sirens and a hovering helicopter all contributed to a deafening welcome. My son Ron joined me as I headed the lengthy column of people and vehicles towards the beckoning tape. The turntable ladder and the pump escape ladder formed an inverted 'V' to create an arch for me to pass beneath. The crowds were immense.

With Mayor and Chief Howells, Swasie at 'Land's End' sign

In my wildest dreams I did not expect such a tumultuous welcome. A helicopter hovered overhead as I breasted the tape and passed beneath a large banner bearing the words 'Well Done Swasie'. I was grabbed and hugged by everyone. I was having difficulty taking in what was going on. Fire Chief Mick Howells shook my hand and everyone screamed and shouted. It was sheer, delightful and ecstatic pandemonium. My son Ron gave me a hug and put his lips to my ear and shouted, 'Well done Dad, I'm proud of you'. This gesture brought the tears rolling down my cheeks. I couldn't contain my emotions any longer. There at the front of the crowd was Matron, snapping away furiously with her camera to record for posterity such

Crossing the finishing line

a crowning welcome. I was truly overwhelmed. The Mayor of Cornwall took my hand and pumped it vigorously as he congratulated me on my mammoth achievement. The wonderful Cilla George and her colleagues from the Land's End to John O'Groats Company came to greet me warmly and take a number of photographs.

Without the help, blessing and advice from Cilla and her 'end-to-end' organisation the whole endeavour could not have been the total success that it was.

I will be eternally grateful to Cilla for her tireless help, expertise and kind assistance, which ensured the ultimate success of the

Signing in at Land's End

Swasie and a proud 'Matron', Land's End Hotel

'mission'. I am now very privileged to include such a wonderful lady as Cilla among my close and valued friends.

After having to 'sign in' to officially record my lengthy endeavour, I was guided to the 'Land's End' signpost for formal Fire Brigade, Lomax, press and media pictures to be taken. Once this formal procedure was successfully concluded we all adjourned to the nearby Land's End Hotel. Here, yet more pleasant surprises continued to unfold. A large and varied mouth-watering buffet took up a major portion of the big room, which overlooked the sea. Finally our large party sat at the previously set tables. The gathering of police and fire personnel, their senior officers, local dignitaries and officials from various associations were called to order. First, the Mayor gave a formal address of welcome. This was followed by an equally warm and enthusiastic welcoming speech by Cilla George. Chief Fire Officer, Mick Howells then gave a similar inspiring address. Mr John Wilmot then addressed the large assembly. His chest swelled with pride as he gave his welcoming rhetoric, revelling in the virtues his factory's product, *my wheelchair*, a *standard* product of such high quality that it could not be equalled!

I was presented with various trophies and gifts from each of the speakers.

Cilla George announced that the chair would be placed on permanent display in the nearby prestigious 'end-to-end' museum, (where it now takes pride of place). My nearly 1000 mile wheelchair push in 44 days is officially the first such journey to have been undertaken and successfully completed, unaided, in an ordinary, castered NHS wheelchair.

Mr Wilmot and his wife Careen concluded this most enjoyable and truly memorable day by hosting a lavish celebratory dinner in my honour at our final overnight's accommodation, the luxurious Queens Hotel in Penzance.

On Sunday, 2nd July, the 45th day after setting out from John O'Groats, I travelled home from Penzance and enjoyed the comforts of being a front seat passenger in Chris's big 4x4 Trooper. I sat and admired the beautiful scenery during my 300-mile journey home.

There was yet another surprise as I arrived at my Wirral home. My daughter Jo had been extremely busy arranging and catering for a big 'Welcome Home' party. A large banner stretched across the front of the house bearing the words, 'WELL-DONE DAD, YOU DID IT'.

As I entered the house the well-known, American World heavyweight boxer Ernie Shavers greeted me. He shook my hand and congratulated me on my success. The house was *full* of friends and relatives, some of whom I hadn't seen for many years. My thoughtful daughter Jo had gone to great lengths to ensure yet another extremely warm welcome home. She did extremely well in bringing about such a large gathering of friends and relatives.

The buffet was stunning. A large cake with the words 'Congratulations Swasie' had pride of place in the centre of the table. Champagne corks popped and finally, in walked Art, the 'other half' of our successful team. I thought he had left for Scotland when we left the Land's End Hotel. The party went on into the early hours. We didn't need to worry about disturbing my neighbours as most of them had joined us and were busy celebrating too!

Jo's cake for Dad's arrival home

Swasie and Ernie Shavers

My jubilation, however, was tinged with my ongoing sadness, – if *only* my beloved Marje could share my success, a success which is continually being brought about because **she alone** is the *total* inspiration for all my endeavours!

Epilogue

AFTER THIS PHENOMENAL 'end-to-end' success, Swasie's chair now resides inside the 'end-to-end' museum at Land's End for all to see. This long distance push in a *standard* NHS castered wheelchair is still an unequalled 'First'.

At no time during the lengthy journey was the chair subject to any form of repair or maintenance (with the exception of a faulty mileometer replacement) and the distance was completed on the same set of front and rear tyres from start to finish.

Subsequently a formal cheque presentation was later held at the Lomax Factory in Dundee where the Lady Provost presented Miss Jan Hayes, Fund Co-ordinator for the Clatterbridge Cancer Research Trust with a cheque for £7,000. A cheque for an equal amount was presented to the Fire Brigades National Benevolent Fund. Due to the ongoing donations as the result of the successful endeavour, contributions to the two charities involved were ongoing for a long time afterwards.

Since Swasie's push, an official 'end-to-end' celebration and trophy presentation was held by the Land's End to John O'Groats Company at the Land's End Hotel. This was for those who had completed the journey and were deemed worthy of an award. Swasie received the prestigious 'President's Trophy' award from the company's Mr Kevin Leech. The large, handsome cup (and an accompanying silver salver for him to keep) was in recognition of him having completed the mammoth distance in 'a most inventive' way! (Category E).

After completing his 'end-to-end' push, Swasie has gone on to push across the inhospitable and unforgiving terrain of the Falkland

Art, Swas, Grant and Dundee Lady Provost

Islands (both East and West islands) where he raised a considerable amount for both the Clatterbridge Cancer Campaign (who actually treat cancer patients from the Falkland Islands) and the South Atlantic Medal Association (Falkland Veterans). On his return to England he again applied to participate in the London Marathon, informing them that if he was again refused he would seek redress via the 'Discrimination against the Disabled Act' through the courts. This time, he *was* allowed to enter and he completed the event without difficulty, nor was he in *any* way 'a danger or hindrance to others taking part'! He sincerely hopes that his setting a precedent for ordinary NHS wheelchair users will be an inspiration for others to follow in his 'tracks'. For a complete update as to Swasie's ongoing and future endeavours, go to www.swasieturner.org

Miles of Memories Museum, home of Swasie's chair with Cilla George

Synopsis

SINCE THE TRAUMATIC loss of both his police career and his right leg due to an act of violence in the line of duty, which has left him confined to a wheelchair, Swasie then suffered the inconsolable loss of his beloved wife and childhood sweetheart Marjorie to the scourge of cancer.

Totally devastated by the death of his beloved wife and lifelong sweetheart, Swasie then decided to raise money to fight the indiscriminate killer amongst us. He became a relentless, dedicated and totally *obsessive* crusader for this cause. Right from the start, against medical advice, he performed unbelievable feats of strength and stamina with his castered, standard issue NHS Lomax wheelchair. Since his wheelchair confinement from February 1997 Swasie has successfully completed the following – *ALL* with his trusty wheelchair, and all being 'firsts':

Ascended to the top of   Leasowe Lighthouse, Wirral
   New Brighton Lighthouse, Wallasey
   Talacre Lighthouse, North Wales
   Pembroke Lighthouse, East Falkland Island
   Blackpool Tower
   Wallace Monument, Stirling.

Pushed (three miles each way) across the sands of the Dee Estuary to Hilbre Island and back.

Pushed 41 miles non-stop from Talacre, North Wales, to his home in Wirral in 11 hrs 30 mins.

Pushed 72 miles non-stop around the coastal roads of the Island of Anglesey in 20 hours.

Pushèd non-stop, the 38 mile Isle of Man TT motor cycle race course in 11 hrs 40 mins.

Pushed the annual 15 mile cross country Wirral 'Walk' 4 times.

Pushed the annual 26 mile 'Egg Run' 3 times (A motor cycle event).

Pushed the London Marathon.

Pushed the Robin Hood Marathon.

Pushed 60 miles non-stop from Christie Cancer Hospital, Manchester to Clatterbridge (Cancer Research) Hospital, Wirral in 12 hrs 40 mins.

Pushed to every fire station in the Merseyside Fire Brigade area, 110 miles in 4 days.

Pushed John O'Groats to Land's End, 904.2 miles in 44 days.

Pushed the 26 mile 'Windsor Walk' (which is only for able-bodied police and ex-police officers from all European countries).

Pushed across East Falkland Island from Port San Carlos to Stanley (72 miles) retracing 3 Commando Brigade and 2 Para's wartime trek in 4 days and 4 nights.

Pushed East Falkland Island from Mount Pleasant to Stanley (32 miles). Pushed across West Falkland Island from Fox Bay to Port Howard, 82 miles.

Pushed 500 miles from Stroud, Gloucs to Dudestacht near to what was once the East German border.

Pushed 7 miles across the tropical island of Ascension and to the top of Green Mountain (3,017ft) thus completing the island's 'Dew Pond Run'.

Pushed 286 miles from the Whitehouse, Washington DC to New York's Ground Zero.

Swasie has also completed numerous other smaller pushes for local charities.

Pushed 210 miles from Wallasey Town Hall, Wirral to Buckingham Palace with congratulatory messages (and receiving donations for the F.S.N.B.F.) for Her Majesty the Queen during her Golden Jubilee year of 2002.

Swasie's ultimate endeavour was being awarded the coveted Royal Marines' Green Beret after completing the arduous Commando Endurance course at Lympstone, Devon. This was then followed by an ascent of Ben Nevis with the Royal Marines. Further pushes then were the 172 mile Leeds to Liverpool canal towpath.

A 108 mile push from Badwater to Townes Pass through the arid and inhospitable 'Death Valley', Nevada. For this Swasie was awarded the Key to the City of Las Vegas by Mayor Oscar B. Goodman as well as a prestigious silver medal from the Governor of Nevada.

During the 'European Year for Disabled People' (2003) Swasie set off from Westminster Parliament, when he was seen off by Maria Eagle, the Minister for Disabled, and pushed his chair to the European Parliament in Brussels. This push raised funds for the disabled people of Europe as well as creating awareness of those who are physically handicapped.

April 2004 saw Swasie ascend the awesome and infamous 'Jacob's Ladder' on the tropical island of Saint Helena. This is a set of 700 steps rising beyond 45 degrees, 900 feet of a cliff face. The climb raised thousands of pounds for the Saint Helena Hospital.

As well as regularly attending the Royal Marines' Training Centre at Lympstone, Devon to assist in the inspiration of injured recruits by accompanying those recovering from injuries on their marches, Swasie has just completed another daunting and physically demanding endeavour. He has recently successfully completed the 32 mile distance 'Exe Descent' canoe endeavour from Tiverton to Exeter along the fast flowing, dangerous waters of the River Exe again with the Royal Marines.

To date, Swasie has pushed his chair a total of 33,400 miles and raised over half a million pounds for various worthy causes and charities, – each and every endeavour is *all in memory of his beloved wife Marjorie.*

For his unique services to charity, Swasie was given the ultimate accolade on being made an MBE in Her Majesty the Queen's 2005 birthday honours.